W9-CQN-177

The greatest resource America has is her people. The most precious gift in all the world is human life. The greatest good is to serve your fellowman. The greatest tragedy is the refusal of American people to get involved on behalf of those who will come after us.

— DON WILDMON, 1982

I HAD A VISION.
GOD HAD A PLAN.

※

DONALD E. WILDMON

WITH ALLEN WILDMON

Copyright © 2013 Donald E. Wildmon

All Rights Reserved

This book may not be reproduced, transmitted, or stored in whole or in part by any means, including graphic, electronic, or mechanical without the express written consent of the publisher except in the case of brief quotations embodied in critical articles and reviews.

 Cover design by Rusty Benson

All quotes from the Bible are from the King James Version. The chapters of this book are not necessarily in chronological order.

ISBN: 978-0-615-80843-7

AMERICAN FAMILY ASSOCIATION
Tupelo, Mississippi
www.afa.net

Printed in the United States of America by Signature Book Printing, www.sbpbooks.com

This book is available at store.afa.net or by calling 662-844-5036.

DEDICATED TO

My wife, Lynda; my sons, Tim and Mark; my daughters, Donna and Angela, and to all the supporters of the American Family Association who have stood shoulder to shoulder with me in the cultural war over the years

CONTENTS

Contents

Contents

Section 5: Appendix –What We Are Up Against

Preface

More than two thousand years ago a Man named Christ said, "If the world hates you, keep in mind that it hated me first." And so it was with Don Wildmon in his more than thirty-year battle for traditional values. He got a touch of that hatred quite often.

The three television networks, ABC, CBS, NBC, the secular news media, The American Humanist Association, People For The American Way, Americans for the Separation of Church and State, the Southern Poverty Law Center, the ACLU and the pornography industry all had a little hate to throw his way.

Playboy magazine once sent a reporter to Tupelo to dig up dirt on Don. The reporter spent two weeks in Don's hometown. It was a waste of money. The reporter gave up and went home.

When the anti-Christian movement found they couldn't debate him based on truth and facts, they tried to use character assassination. That did not work, either. They painted him as an extreme, rightwing fundamentalist and an uneducated Bible-toting, Scripture-quoting, ignorant redneck preacher who was trying to force his morals on everyone else. His enemies soon found that he was none of those.

He actually helped them believe that portrayal. He said it helped to get those opposing him to underestimate him. He was a well-read traveler with a Bachelor degree from Millsaps College in Jackson, Mississsippi, and a Masters degree from Emory University in Atlanta. He also was recognized with honorary doctor degrees from two well respected universities, Wesley Biblical Seminary in Jackson, Mississippi and Asbury College in Wilmore, Kentucky. He also had plenty of common sense, something which many in the media lacked.

Some examples of the name calling he received over the years and their sources were: Bob Merilis, spokesperson for Warner Brothers studios, called Don a Crypto Snake Handler (a person who handles snakes in a secret or hidden place). The name implies Don was one of those preachers who handled snakes while standing in a church pulpit. *Playboy* magazine called Don A Religious Dingbat. The American Gay Atheist Association referred to the American Family Association as The American Facifist Association. *Adult Video News*, the folks who promote hardcore pornography, called him The Lunatic Fringe Player in the First Amendment Suppression Game. *New Age Magazine* called him a Huckster and the Philadelphia Gay Press referred to him as a Dangerous Demagogue. *Hustler* magazine gave him their monthly award, which placed his picture on the south end of a horse traveling north; its tail held high in the air. James Rosenfield, president of CBS network, referred to Don as the Ayatollah of the Religious Right. Gene Mater, vice-president of CBS, called Don the "greatest threat to intellectual freedom this country has ever seen."

Next, they tried to make the American people think Don was a "censor," that is one who decided what the public would see on television and read in magazines. Don would remind the public the real censors were the networks themselves. Every show on television has been censored by those who put it on the air. He called the public's attention to the fact that Christians were rarely depicted on television, and when they were, it was nearly always in a negative light. He challenged the networks to name a single program, set in a modern timespan, which depicted a Christian in a positive manner.

The editor of the local newspaper wrote an editorial calling Don a censor because **The Last Temptation of Christ** was not shown locally.

The editor could drive to another community to see the movie if he desired. But no, he had rather complain because he could not walk across the street to see the film. How could a person be a censor when more than 100 theatres were showing the "censored" movie? The local editor wanted to censor Don's right to protest while crying freedom of speech for himself. Only the government can censor. Remember that the next time someone cries censor.

Don often stated that the networks could show what they desire, the viewer could watch what he desires, and the individual can spend his money where he desires. It is hard to find censorship in that proposal. Having studied the networks for over thirty years, Don has learned one thing; the networks are motivated by money and ideology.

In the leftwing's attempt to destroy Don, little did they know they were helping build one of the nation's largest and strongest pro-family Christian organizations – the American Family Association. The secular left's failure in their attempt to destroy Don's character actually had little to do with Don Wildmon. He wasn't the ultimate target of their denigration. The removal of Christian influence from American society is their goal.

It is our intent to introduce you to the real Don Wildmon by sharing information of a personal nature, information not reported in the liberal media.

– ALLEN WILDMON, *Don's brother*

SECTION ONE

Setting the Stage

I

Ten minutes into our first date I tell Lynda I will marry her

In the summer of 1960, I met Lynda Bennett. She attended Northeast Mississippi Community College and was a cheerleader for the basketball team and a Campus Beauty. She completed her undergraduate education at Mississippi University for Women, generally referred to as the "W" and earned her Master's degree in Home Economics from the University of Mississippi.

When I first asked her for a date, she told me she had to study for a chemistry test. Her parents, like the Wildmons who had to watch their money, were paying for summer classes and she felt she absolutely had to pass chemistry. About a week later I asked her again. This time she agreed.

If she had declined again, the story would have ended there. I had a standing rule that if I was turned down twice I did not ask again. I said I was smart enough to know when a girl was not interested.

On our first date, with Lynda being in the car for maybe 10 minutes, I looked across the seat and spoke: "I think I will marry you." Lynda didn't respond, but later asked herself a question, "What have I got myself into?"

It was on our second date I shared a secret with her. I told her God had something for me to do, but I did not yet know what it was.

After we were married one year later, on nearly the same day as our first date, we moved into a mobile home in Columbus, Mississippi, and began to settle down. Lynda was a senior at the "W" and I was an insurance agent. But Uncle Sam had other ideas.

I was drafted and told to report for duty. While Lynda went to live in the dormitory, I went to Fort Leonard Wood, Missouri. I spent 21 months serving in the U.S. Army, all of them at Fort Leonard Wood. My duties in the army were with Special Services. Don't confuse Special Services with Special Forces. Special Services operated such activities as golf, basketball, skating rink, movies, etc.

At the time I was drafted, I was a licensed Methodist minister. As such, I was exempt from the draft. I was approached by an older minister who was my superintendent. He offered to hire me as his associate if I wished. I had not yet turned in my ministerial papers. I was still eligible to be exempt from serving.

I told my superintendent I appreciated the offer, but felt I should refuse it. "Why should I be exempt? I am no different than others who have fought and died," I told him.

As a teenager, I felt God was calling me into the parish ministry as a pastor. I was licensed by my denomination and enrolled in Millsaps College to prepare for the parish ministry. After I graduated in 1960, I accepted the position as pastor of three small churches and basketball coach at a small junior college.

For the next year, while serving as a pastor, I struggled with my calling. I resigned my position with the small churches and the junior college. I was very frustrated. I knew God had something for me to do, but I still did not know what. It was a feeling that would be with me from the age of nine to the age of thirty-nine.

While in the army, one Sunday I skipped the chapel service and instead sat down under a big oak tree on the hillside opposite my army barracks. I needed to do some serious thinking, praying, listening and talking with God concerning my future. Ever since I had accepted Christ as a nine-year-old, I had a feeling God had something for me to do.

And now, at age twenty-three, I still did not know what God wanted me to do with my life.

For some time I sat beneath that tree, praying and listening. As I listened, it became clear what God was saying to me and it wasn't something I wanted to hear. God was telling me to go back into the parish ministry. I had no desire to go back into the parish ministry. Nothing had changed, and it was yet to come that I would learn the meaning of God's grace.

I left the hillside that Sunday morning with a clear message I was to prepare myself to become a parish minister. That meant I should make plans to enroll at Emory University's Candler School of Theology in Atlanta. However, Emory told me my grades from Millsaps College indicated I could not pass their work.

Emory would not approve my application because, in their opinion, I could not do the work at the level they required. Emory had good reason to believe I could not pass their work.

In my years at Millsaps, I made the Dean's List two times. The first time I made the Dean's List, it was the academic probation list. I had a semester to make my grades or I would be gone. During that semester I studied much more than I had during the previous semester. I not only passed my work to get off academic probation, I made the good Dean's List due to my high grades. I may very well be the only student at Millsaps which went from the bad Dean's List to the good Dean's List in one semester.

Another hurdle I faced in graduating from Millsaps was my required science classes. I had taken Botany in my first semester in college at Mississippi State, where I spent my first semester in college. I had to take the second semester of Botany in order to graduate. So my final semester at Millsaps I took the second semester of Botany. I was never good in science and taking the second semester of Botany in my final semester was beyond my ability. I remember on my first test in the Botany class I made a score of thirty-seven. Yes, thirty-seven.

I struggled the entire semester. I remember on my final test I made sixty-eight which was an F. Seventy would have been a D and a passing grade. I went to the professor and pleaded my case. He was not sympathetic. He suggested I take the course during the summer. I explained that my parents had funded my college work and I didn't think it right to ask them to fund even more.

Millsaps had the reputation of being tough academically. But failing me over two points on a course which I would never use in the real world and taking the second part four years after I took the first part just didn't make sense. I went to my advisor to discuss the situation. He told me of a rule for graduating seniors. It was this: If a senior scheduled to graduate failed a course, the student would be allowed to take a separate test and if the student passed the test, he or she would be allowed to graduate.

I took the test. Whether I passed the test or the professor simply gave me a passing grade, I don't know. My inclination tells me the professor gave me a passing grade. The grades were posted on the bulletin board outside his office. There was a single word beside my name - passed.

Now, back to the refusal of Emory to admit me. My next move was to ask two influential friends for help. One was a member of the school's Board and the other was a wealthy lawyer who gave money to Emory. I asked these friends to write Emory on my behalf. They wrote and asked Emory to accept my application. The chairman of the admissions committee replied explaining why my application to enroll was refused.

"I know they (Emory) will do everything they possibly can to work it out for him (Don). On the other hand if, after he takes the tests, it appears he will be in an impossible situation. It would probably be best for him as well as the school to pass on the matter.

"I am sure you realize when a boy gets in a school where he is completely over his head, it creates a sense of frustration rather than help. Anyway, I hope it will work out. We deeply appreciate your interest in this matter." After much communication, Emory agreed to give me a test and if I passed the test, they would accept my application. I passed the test. You could say I had to take a test to get out of Millsaps and a test to get into Emory.

I finished Emory in two years and three summers. The normal time it took to graduate was three years. On a four point scale, I finished my work at Emory with a 3.2 [B+ A-] grade average.

To help pay the bills while in seminary, I accepted the pastorate at a church about forty miles from Atlanta. Four days a week, I would leave home about 6:30 a.m. with three other ministerial students. I finally decided I could not do the work as pastor of a church while a full-time student. So we decided to move on campus.

However, there was a little more about the move than work load. There was a lady in the church who was evidently bored with my sermons. She would sit on the second pew and read her magazines while I was preaching. One Sunday I brought several magazines with me. Just before I was to preach, I gave them to her. "Here are some more magazines if you run out," I said. Would I do something like that again? Probably not.

Our campus apartment had a large 12 x 15 room, a smaller 10 x 8 room, and a 6 x 6 kitchen. I could walk to my classes and Lynda had the use of the car if she needed it. She worked one morning a week at a mother's day out at a church not too distant from the Emory Campus. Lynda was paid $15 and could bring our two children at no cost. When we moved to Tupelo she opened the first mother's morning out in the city.

On Sundays, after church, I would take Lynda and the two children to eat out about a mile from the Emory campus. It was a new restaurant named McDonald's. We could eat there for less than a dollar. Lynda, Tim and I got a hamburger (10¢), Coke (10¢) and French fries (12¢). Total: (96¢). (Angela was still on baby food.)

After we moved to the apartment on campus, I worked carrying out groceries at a Kroger store nearby. I worked on minimum wage plus tips. I once got a $20 tip. That was a really big time tip. Despite not having much money, we decided to take a short trip to Florida. Rounding up all the money we could find, including literally breaking the piggy bank and getting the change – even including the nickels and dimes - we managed to accumulate $78. We left for Florida, about 200 miles away, for a three day vacation. We had about $5 left when we got home. We had a good time despite not having much money. The beach was free. And so were many of the sites.

When I finished my studies and we moved back to Mississippi, we owed a total of $4,500. That happened to be exactly the amount of my first year's salary. Lynda stayed home until she took a teaching position and taught during the 1966/1967 school year. It was a difficult position. She decided to stay home and take care of not one, not two, but three little children.

I was appointed by my bishop to serve three small churches in Tishomingo County in northeast Mississippi. Lynda and I had a good ministry in the three years we served the churches. We got to know some really lovely people. One Christmas they gave us a money tree. It was a small Christmas tree with money bills pinned on the tree. It had about $100 on it. It may not seem like much, but at that time it was a nice gift. It also showed their appreciation for us.

Our first year there Lynda and I bought an 8mm camera and projector. We bought it on our newly acquired Sears Credit Card. I took the camera and visited every member's home. While there I took pictures of the members while they were doing something in the way of usual chores around the house. I took the film and spliced it together. Then I wrote a script and recorded the script and put music in the background. We planned a big night at the church and showed the homemade movie. It was a little unusual, but the members enjoyed it.

Another project I took on while we were serving in Tishomingo County was starting a worship service at a state park near our parsonage. The park was located on a large lake with hundreds of lakeside homes. Since it was my first church service to preach at on Sunday morning and it was on the way to another of my churches, I could work it in my preaching schedule. I put up a sign at the pavilion and passed out brochures in the immediate area. The first Sunday we had a good crowd. In about a month we had a crowd of about seventy-five. Many of those attending the worship service at the lake lived in Tupelo and came up to their vacation homes on the weekend, I would meet many of them again when we moved to Tupelo to build a new church.

After serving the three churches for a few months, I arranged the time for worship services so each church could have a Sunday morning service. I preached at 9:00, 10:00 and 11:00. Our parsonage was in the middle of two of the churches. Lynda knew what time I would be at the parsonage to get her and the children. You could say Sundays were a busy day for us. On some Sundays Lynda would take all three children to all services. The church members wanted to see the children. Lynda always brought some cookies, candy and small toys. And the children were well behaved. She sat on the back pew.

We did enjoy our people in those three churches, and the ones at the park. Lynda and I were blessed in many ways by the churches we served. But there was the dark side. The mid-sixties were a time when the civil rights battle was at the forefront. I tried to lead my congregations toward reconciliation, an effort in which my denomination was very much involved. One night, when the family and I were out attending a church service, we were reminded someone didn't appreciate our stand. When we got home, there was a note from the KKK pinned on our small bulletin board in the hall of the parsonage. Someone had entered the house and left the note while we were gone. We did not lock our doors in those days.

Tim, our first born, entered this world on March 6, 1963 in Houston, Missouri, while I was still in the army. On March 6, 1964 our daughter Angela was born at Cartersville, Georgia, while I was in seminary. The fact they had the same birthday brought plenty of notice. Every time Lynda and I had to furnish their birth certificates there was always that pause, and then the eye contact with the person. And we always had to say, "Yes, they have the same birthday."

When Angela was born, I had a bet for a steak dinner with another ministerial student I carpooled with that she would be born on March 6. I got a free steak dinner out of the deal.

When Donna was born on February 1, it took away some of the disbelief. But it quickly resumed when Mark was born on March 6, 1971. When asked why we had three children born on the same day, Lynda and I told them we were cutting down on the birthday parties by having them all on one day.

2

Turn the Television Off Week gets off the ground

In 1968, after serving three small Methodist churches for three years, our family moved to Tupelo, Mississippi, a city of about 40,000 which has been an All-American city four times in the past 30 years. I had asked my bishop to be appointed to a new church in Tupelo, Lee Acres United Methodist Church. I told my friends all I wanted was a plot of ground and a place for my family to live. I was given a new parsonage and four acres of land.

My friends told me that taking the Lee Acres appointment was not a good idea. Even my superintendent (boss) tried to talk me out of it. Each of the other Methodist ministers in Tupelo told me it was a bad situation.

I learned that truth when I arrived. The church had already constructed a building. It was a 20 x 40 plywood building with one room, no water, no windows, no toilet and no insulation. In Mississippi in the summer it gets pretty hot. The building had metal seats. Sunday school was held in a home across the street from where the church's plywood building was located. And if that were not enough, the church had no money and only a handful of members.

After I had been at the church about three months, the church rented space from a school. For the next two years we would meet in the school building. It was difficult for me and the handful of members to recruit new members.

Before the church was built, I had no pastor's study. But I did have a utility room under the carport at the parsonage. The utility room measured about 6 x 8 feet and worked as a study just fine. I managed to get my books, typewriter, radio, telephone and other items in the study. There was room for only one person. Using the storage room as a study did not concern me. It worked just fine. From time to time our five-year-old Tim would come into the small study and sit for a while. When Tim would ask me what I was doing when he would stop by, I would tell him I was studying. One time when he came into the study, he picked up a book, a pencil and some paper. After he had been real quiet for some time, I asked him what he was doing. His reply? "I'm studying."

After two years, with money from the conference and the members, the church built a 5000 square foot metal building. It wasn't the most beautiful building in the city, but it was reasonably attractive. Many did not like it. The mayor called the metal building the "tin can on the hill." The building didn't bother me. I considered the people to be the church, not the building. But the building did bother others and did nothing to help recruit new members.

I stayed at the church eight years. I put my heart and soul into the church. I didn't exactly set the world on fire in those eight years. I worked hard, but the growth of the church was slow. At the end of eight years, the church had a membership of seventy-five with an average of seventy-three in the morning worship service.

Some of the reasons for the low membership were a direct result of my leadership. One wanting to join the church must have been attending regularly for six months and assume a position to apply one's talents. Sunday school teachers were rotated each three months and members were encouraged to tithe.

Compared to standards for all churches, the church had the highest percentage of worship attendance in the conference and the highest per capita giving in the conference.

Below is a message for the potential church member which was published on the back of the church bulletin.

From the minister: A note to the prospective member of Lee Acres Church

The vows of church membership are among the most serious vows one can take. They should not be entered into lightly. Before pledging one's life to Christ, one should examine the demands Christ makes.

Too often church membership vows are not taken seriously. That is a sin against both those who do take their membership seriously and against Christ, the Head of the church. It is far better not to take the vows than to take them and not do so seriously.

Every member of the church has certain duties and responsibilities as well as rights. Far too often, the rights are expounded and the responsibilities neglected.

Every member should expect from the church certain obligations. The church has a duty to serve its members as well as its community and world. The church should provide a place of love, help and concern for its members. But in a like manner, the church has an equal right to expect members to support the church with their prayers, their presence, their gifts and their service. It also has the right to expect a serious study of the New Testament both from its members and prospective members.

As minister of this church when one asks for membership in this church I expect this membership will be taken seriously. Before joining the church, one should be fully aware of the commitment it requires. I ask not that the candidate be perfect in faith or churchmanship. Such a request would be foolish. But what I do ask is there be a genuine and serious concern for and love of the church and Christ.

One should never join the church simply to be "joining the church." One should do so because of the great love Christ expressed for all people and the church at Calvary's cross.

If you wish to take membership seriously, let's talk. If membership is a casual thing, visit with us often.

Donald E. Wildmon, Pastor

Feeling I was holding the church back, and still lacking a clear vision of what "special ministry" God wanted me to do, in early summer of 1976 I asked to be moved. I was assigned to Southaven United Methodist Church in the suburbs of Memphis, Tennessee.

In my eight years in Tupelo, I never lost the feeling God had something "special" for me to do. But the flame had grown dim over the years, and I had just about felt it go out. After all, it was thirty years ago when I began searching for God's will. While serving churches for the past thirteen years, I was somewhat bored and felt constrained. I felt like a monkey in a cage, going round and round and getting nowhere.

One night during the Christmas holidays in 1976, the family gathered in front of the TV. I asked one of the children to see what was on the channels. At this time in 1976 there were only three networks: NBC, CBS, and ABC. As the channels were being viewed, here is what they had as choices: One man had another tied down and was hitting him with a hammer; another showed two people, obviously not married, in bed; and on the third channel was a man using profanity. I asked one of the children to turn the set off.

Angry, I started thinking how this could be changed. I knew television was having a negative effect on society. But how do you change a multi-billion dollar industry?

That night, while lying in bed, I was thinking of some way I could get the attention of the networks. I came up with the idea of a campaign asking my church members and others across the country to join in observing Turn The Television Off Week (TTOW). The next Sunday morning I preached on the negative influence television was having on our society and at the end of the sermon invited the members to participate in TTOW, March 8, 1977.

I also knew this was my "special" ministry for which I had been waiting thirty years.

I felt good about the opportunities the strategy would offer. I had some experience in journalism. The idea was completely unique. The event was planned with plenty of time to promote. It was going to be another David and Goliath battle.

I had journalistic experience going back to my high school days when I wrote sports for a handful of small papers. I had also served as sports editor for my college newspaper. I had a weekly religious column which ran in nearly 500 papers. I had helped establish a general circulation weekly newspaper.

I began TTOW efforts with a press release which I mailed to all the media outlets in Memphis. I also took the press release to the Associated Press office in downtown Memphis. I chatted a little with the reporter on duty and explained what I was doing and why. I shook hands with the reporter and went to the hospital in Memphis to do some visitation. While in the hospital visiting, I called my secretary to see if I had any messages. She said all the television stations and other media in Memphis were calling wanting an interview with me.

I headed back to the church. When the news came on the radio the next hour, TTOW led the newscast. The battle had begun.

I had no budget and no money. How then did I publicize TTOW? Here is what columnist Marilynn Preston of the Chicago Tribune, wrote: "I admit it," he (Don) laughed. I used as many gimmicks as I could in the beginning. I had no money, no organization. What could I do?" Preston reported, "He did plenty." He sent a telegram to all the governors in the country asking for their support. He wired President Carter asking for his support. Only the governors of Hawaii and Michigan expressed any real interest. Finally the Associated Press picked up the story and like sticking a match to a firecracker, a loud noise by the nation's media began."

My ability to get my ideas across would become a major asset or American Family Association. The two largest secular trade publications in America honored my efforts. *Ad Week* named me the Marketer of the Year in 1981. *Advertising Age* listed me as one of ten top people who made a mark on marketing in 2004. Joining me on being honored were Karl Rove, Mel Gibson and Lance Armstrong.

After TTOW was over, I resigned my pastorate and moved the family back to Tupelo. The American Family Association was born.

3
Searching 30 years for the purpose of my life

When I was nine years old, I attended a revival service in my home church. The preacher was Rev. Smoot. I don't remember what Rev. Smoot said in his sermon, but I do remember when the invitation was given, I went forward and gave my life to Jesus. After the service, I felt God had a plan for me. I didn't know what it was, but I believed He did have something for me to do, something "special." For the next 30 years I kept feeling God had something "special" for me to do.

In 1951 there was a young evangelist going around the country holding crusade meetings. The services were held in a tent. His preaching, a straight-forward, no-nonsense approach, began drawing good sized crowds. The head of one of the largest newspaper chains in America heard the evangelist preach and told his editors to "puff" the evangelist. The publisher, William Randolph Hearst, gave the young preacher good coverage, increasing the size of the crowds wherever he preached.

The traveling evangelist put up his tent in Memphis. The crowds were mostly receptive to his message. A 13-year-old skinny kid was in the audience one night during the crusade. He listened to the sermon with intensity.

When the sermon ended and the invitation was given to those who wanted to rededicate their life to come forward, the 13-year-old kid got up and walked down the aisle. All who came forward were taken to the back of the tent where they were given counseling and reading material. The evangelist at that revival meeting was a young preacher named Billy

Graham. The 13-year-old kid was Don Wildmon.

The experience helped confirm my belief that God had something special for me to do with my life.

I rarely said in public God had something special for me to do. The reason I rarely used the word special in public was that I feared someone would feel that special meant something bigger and better than the task God had called them to do. My pursuit of that to which I felt God had called me was a long journey down many paths. First was the feeling God wanted me to be a missionary to China.

As I grew older I finally decided that special thing was being an ordained minister. I accepted my first appointment as a minister at age 21 while I was still a student in college.

The burning flame I had in the past was slowly dying. Maybe God didn't have something special for me to do. I felt God calling me back into the parish ministry. I went back and spent 13 years in the parish ministry.

Finally, at age 39, God showed me what He had for me. It was to found and grow American Family Association. I knew without any doubt AFA was what He had in store for me. It was that special calling. I never doubted; AFA was the mission God had planned for me. As I look back, I see that at each bend in the road, when it appeared I was taking the wrong turn, He was preparing me to do His will in my life.

I had a vision. God had a plan.

4

Society is in a slow moral meltdown

Whatever labels you use to describe the driving philosophical road in our society today – liberal, progressive, leftwing, etc. – they all lead back to secular humanism. It is a godless religion which Christians desperately need to study. It is a religion of which only a handful of individuals have heard. The Christian community needs to learn what secular humanism is, and how it is finding acceptance and promotion in our society, even among some Christians. The religion of secular humanism goes directly to the base of Christianity, seeking to destroy it. For that reason I have included a study of this godless religion in this book.

When I first started AFA, I thought I was fighting profanity, sex and violence on television. But over the next few years I came to the conclusion what was happening was a battle against Western Civilization, which came from the mind of Christ and gave us the foundation for our law and culture. Those who came to this country were seeking freedom, especially freedom of religion. They came to build a new country, a country founded on the Christian religion. The writings of those early settlers indicated how deep their faith was. But for a country founded by faithful Christians, we have moved far, far away.

I am often asked if America is a Christian nation. When we speak of America being a Christian nation, we must clarify our response. If one means our nation today is a Christian nation in practice, the answer is no. If one means our nation was founded on the Christian religion, the answer is yes.

The secular mind has made giant inroads in our society in the past half-century. While the rest of America was sleeping, these people were working fast and hard to impose their godless vision on America. And, I might add, they have done a pretty good job of it.

With about 300,000 churches in America, you would think the moral decay we have seen in the last half-century could not happen. But it did. In fact, it continues to grow. And, sadly, for some churches it is not a matter of concern. What is the reason for this? I don't think there is a single reason. I think there is a host of reasons.

One reason is some pastors aren't comfortable preaching on the social issues. Likewise, another reason is many churches don't want their preacher preaching on the social issues. Some preachers believe the most effective way to change the morals of a society is to convert the individual and, to a degree, they are right. Some preachers agree with those pushing us toward a society based on secular humanism.

Some years ago I spoke at a certain church in a certain city. Driving in from the airport, I counted five churches within four blocks of an adult bookstore. But none of the churches had made any effort to oppose the bookstore.

The silence and apathy of the Christian community must end if we are to save our society. We simply must become educated and involved. We must speak out. Our society has suffered too much already because of our silence.

5

Some churches take action
but more are needed

When I began AFA I felt the effort to change television and public morality would take about two to three years. Was I ever wrong! I figured that with about 300,000 to 350,000 churches in America, all we would need to do was to appeal to the churches and they would get involved. I knew to be successful the support of denominations and local churches would be very important. I learned the hard way it was extremely difficult to awaken a sleeping giant.

The place to begin, it seemed to me, was with my own church. A resolution of support was introduced at the annual meeting of my denomination's geographic area. Since I knew just about everyone connected with the Annual Conference, I knew I would get their endorsement. I was not asking for money. When it came time to vote on the resolution, three members who I considered real good friends stood and spoke against it. When the vote for the resolution was called, the conference voted it down.

I was crushed. It was hard for this 40-year-old to hold back tears. I immediately saw my thinking of solving the problem in two to three years was way off base. And it helped me understand what I was up against. But I held on to the belief if enough churches would get involved we could turn the tide. Little did I know what the future held for me.

I purchased a table-top offset press for $400. I knew I would need a lot of printing. Owning an offset press, even a small one, would be a wise investment. There was one problem, however, and that was learning to operate the press. Through trial and error, and a period of several months, I finally learned to use it.

We spent most of the summer of 1977 moving back to Tupelo from Southaven and adjusting to a new routine of life. While Lynda mostly took care of the children, I was beginning to feel my way through my new ministry. I accepted nearly every speaking invitation I was offered, from a few large churches to a lot of small churches and small groups. In fact, I received very little support of any kind from the speaking engagements. Typically, if I spoke in a church with an attendance of 100 people, I would get about 3 or 4 individuals who would sign up to get involved. A year later I would see only one church member that was still active with AFA. You may not believe it, but that was the truth.

My speaking engagements gave me exposure, but little income. To be honest, I'm not sure how we survived those first few years, but we did. By Lynda getting a position teaching home economics, my books and tours, and some help from AFA as funds became available, we made it. Oh, one of the major ways in which we survived was cutting back on our spending. We learned how to cut corners until they were round.

Back to the churches. As I said earlier, I knew the involvement of local churches and denominations would be crucial for success. Churches were the ideal source to carry out the program to fight the decline of morality. They were already organized, had regular meetings, had money to support the fight, and shared with other churches basic morals. Or, at least, I thought they shared the basic morals. AFA was gradually growing and so was our mail. I began getting lots of letters. They were not letters of support. They were letters from pastors who wrote telling me that my efforts, as they related to homosexuality and pornography, were hateful and mean, and I should learn to love other people. As I read the letters, I became aware we were miles apart in theory and interpretation of scripture.

In the early years, I asked several Christian leaders to serve on an Advisory Board. One leader who agreed to be on the Advisory Board was a United Methodist bishop. One of the ministers in his conference wrote the bishop explaining to the bishop why he should not be on my Advisory Board. The bishop wrote back. "I have learned that it is easier to restrain a fanatic than to raise a corpse."

In the 80s we were able to form a coalition of several of the smaller denominations. We were able to make some progress, but the problem kept getting bigger. Over a period of time the coalition gradually lost influence with the smaller denominations. In addition, the situation kept getting worse and worse. Many in pews gradually became desensitized to the world around them. More and more of those church members adopted as their priority going to church, listening to the sermon, and then going home. Unfortunately, many ministers adopted that same philosophy.

I accepted nearly every speaking and media request I received. My travels took me into forty-eight states. These gave me an opportunity to get my message out. The media appearances were always structured in one way. There would be the host (liberal), a person with an opposing view (liberal), and a neutral person (liberal). Nearly everywhere I spoke the audience was three-to-one against me. I was verbally attacked, even in some churches. I had to learn to take the attacks and turn them around. One of the major pluses I had going for me was that I debated on this one issue. It soon came to the place where I had heard all arguments. I always won the debates.

After trying to get churches and pastors involved in the battle, it took about six years for me to realize I was not going to get the support of the vast numbers of churches and pastors. I tried every way I knew to get churches and pastors involved, but to no avail. This had a major effect on me. It took away much of my enthusiasm. I finally quit trying to get churches and pastors involved. I saw it was a waste of time. Of course there were some pastors and churches who saw the battle, but most of them did not. That meant I had to reorient my thinking. Many nights I went to our backyard and pleaded with God to turn me loose and let me do some other kind of work. I would have loved to go to a small church on the back side of nowhere if God would have allowed. But He would not turn me loose from that to which he called me.

SECTION TWO

The Big Night

6
The Gala, a highlight of my life

Saturday, September 18, 2010 was a special day for me and my family, the AFA Board and many employees of AFA. I was honored as the recipient of the James C. Dobson Vision and Leadership Award for my lifetime achievements.

I was honored at a gala dinner that evening, held at the Sheraton hotel in Washington, D.C. with hundreds of Christian leaders present. Tony Perkins, my longtime friend, served as the Master of Ceremonies for the evening. Many of my friends who had fought with me in the cultural war came to the podium one by one and told what I had accomplished over the years.

First there was Dick Bott. He told of the Summer of Mercy when thousands of Christians had come to Wichita, Kansas, to pray and picket because of the babies who were being killed by abortionist Dr. George Tiller. He was one of the few late term abortionists who killed the unborn baby by sucking the baby's brains out while the baby was still in the mother's womb. He was nicknamed "Tiller the killer" and rightly so. In the end he met his own death by a mentally deranged fanatic, Scott Roeder, while attending church.

Following Dick was Dr. James Dobson. He had sent his congratulations by video tape since he couldn't make it in person. He praised my work and pointed out he had met me in 1983 when I did an interview for Focus on The Family radio program. Dr. Dobson, founder of Focus on The Family, said of me, "He never wavered in his war on anti-Christian bias. I drew confidence from him."

Following Dr. Dobson was Janet Parshall. Janet is a well known Christian radio personality and conservative activist. When speaking about me, she said, "I recall the day Don said, 'I simply go where God calls me.'" Janet called me a, "General in the cultural war and a standard bearer who has trained many foot soldiers, and I'm one of them." Speaking to me from only a few feet away, Janet Parshall stated: "Your courage has made millions of Americans more courageous in understanding the nature of the culture war in their own communities ... and more courageous in standing against the evils of our day. In other words, you've taught us about citizenship."

After Janet, Governor Tim Pawlenty of Minnesota, a presidential candidate, spoke very highly of me and my accomplishments by way of video. He apologized for not being there in person, but was with a trade delegation in China.

Next on the program was Congressman Gregg Harper, of the Third District of Mississippi, an attorney who practiced law in Brandon and Ridgeland, Mississippi. He spoke of filling in for Matt Friedeman on American Family Radio's Jackson, Mississippi, station. He told a joke giving the definition of a politician. "Poly"meaning many and "tick" meaning a blood sucking bug. He had covered the West Palm Beach, Florida, (as a volunteer for American Family Radio) presidential recount of votes when the presidential race between George Bush and Al Gore was very close and most of the nation first heard of "hanging chads" and "pregnant chads." A chad was a piece of voting paper which was not completely punched through by a computer used for voting.

Congressman Harper said, "When I contacted Don Wildmon to ask for his endorsement for my congressional race, his reply was, 'Let me think about it.'" He went on to say, "Don doesn't make quick decisions, he wants to pray about it, think about it and then make up his mind." The congressman won his seat. The congressman went on to say, "I would never have been elected without the support of Don Wildmon."

He had only $270,000 in his war chest while his opponent had over one million dollars to spend.

Chuck Colson (October 16, 1931 – April 21, 2012), a past recipient of the award and Founder of the "Prison Fellowship" ministry, was next by video. Chuck touched many lives through his speaking, his books, and engagement with prisoners throughout the nation. He was a Watergate figure who came back from the biggest political scandal of the Nixon era. In the process he became one of the outstanding Christian leaders in America, founding Prison Fellowship, the largest of the world's outreach ministries to prisoners. He described me as someone who deserved the award more than anyone else he could imagine.

"What he has done with his life has been nothing short of remarkable. It's an amazing, amazing story. I don't think there has been a more fearless defender of righteousness and truth than Don Wildmon. Wildmon has an amazing capacity for mobilizing people who will follow him, which is really the definition of what a leader is," Colson said.

Tony Perkins, president of the Family Research Council, the organization sponsoring the Values Voter Summit spoke. Tony had worked for several years alongside me in defense of the unborn and traditional marriage. His actions were often in response to Capitol Hill legislation which affects the nation's families. "I've had the opportunity to work with a number of leaders," Perkins said, "and I just want you to know the example you've been [is one of] serving with humility." That said, the FRC leader said I demonstrated what the Bible says about giving is true. "Because the one who gives, it will be given back to him," Perkins explained. "I have never seen Don Wildmon with a closed hand. I have always seen him with his hand open, willing to give whatever he had to further the movement, to further the cause, to help someone else. And Don, I want you to know that example has not been lost. I hope to be able to follow the example of your leadership. And I know others do as well."

One of my early allies in the pro-family movement was Phyllis

Schlafly with Eagle Forum. She described me as a "tremendous leader" in the conservative pro-family movement who has had a tremendous impact on America. "He's had just a gigantic impact, and it's all for the good," Schlafly shared. "I remember when he started out with his effort to go after some of the advertisers who were advertising on the wrong programs. I thought: 'Well, he's really on to something.'" She used words like "dedicated" and "persevering" to describe me, adding "right on all the issues" as well. "What more could you ask?" Schlafly asked rhetorically.

My son Tim was the last to speak from the podium. Tim had taken over as president of the American Family Association when my illness prevented me from assuming my duties. Tim told the crowd about an altercation he had with the school bully while attending a new school. I told Tim he had every right to defend himself. And he did. Tim had worked at AFA for 23 years at the time of the Gala.

One of those attending the Gala was Matt Barber, now an attorney with Florida-based Liberty Counsel, who shared a story of how I ministered to him personally following a crisis in his professional life several years ago.

Barber explained he was fired by his employer, a Fortune 100 company, after writing an article (on his own time) defending the sanctity of marriage and "pointing out the pitfalls" associated with the homosexual lifestyle. "Don Wildmon found out about my situation, about my circumstances, and I had been fired merely for sharing my faith and my belief in the importance of the family and marriage – and he came rushing to my defense with the entire American Family Association army behind him," he explained. "I've heard from people on the inside. There were over 500,000 emails, letters, and phone calls which came into this corporation," Barber recalled. "We ended up filing a lawsuit and ultimately the lawsuit was settled. Don Wildmon assisted me and my family personally, financially, through the hard times; spiritually he was there to lean on. He really became a mentor to me, and really [became] one of my heroes."

And speaking on behalf of Liberty Counsel, the attorney thanked me "For taking the lead, for stepping forward to take the spears, to take the stones that have been thrown his way, and for standing in the gap for the rest of America. To get beat up the way he has over the years and to just push forward fearlessly in the way he has, he truly is a national resource," continued Barber, "and history will reflect that Don Wildmon is really one of the pioneers, I believe, in the fourth Great Awakening and in the next great revival in this nation."

After the speeches, a video tribute to me followed. After the video ended, Tony, looking at Lynda and me, asked us to come to the stage. I left my table as my children and grandchildren looked on from the crowd. I held my black walking cane in my right hand and walked with a limp toward the stage. I was helped his son-in-law and brother-in-law. When we reached the podium, Tony read the inscription on the award:

"The little town of Dumas, Mississippi, is the home of K and C County Store, Dumas Diner and Pine Grove High School. It is also the hometown of this year's recipient of the Dr. James C. Dobson Vision Leadership Award, Reverend Donald E. Wildmon. Ordained as a United Methodist Minister, the one time member of the Army's Special Services, a former pastor, radio host and commentator, the author of twenty-two books, Don Wildmon has for more than thirty years, demonstrated determination, energy and moral courage we seldom have witnessed in our time; from the founding of the two million member plus American Family Association with 200 plus radio stations, the American Family Radio Network, a major policy (monthly news) Journal and a respected American Family Online Internet Service.

"Don has launched ministries with tremendous reach and effectiveness. Don has been an unwavering example of a servant-leader whose humility made him one of the most outstanding Christian leaders of our time. Don is a man of remarkable vision. Realizing it is not enough to complain about social degradation, he has chosen to fight it, vigorously and strategically. He has not only called for Christians to get involved, he has mobilized them. Don's ministry has not been defined about what he has been against, but rather what he is for, namely the Gospel of our Lord, Jesus Christ; the principles of grace and truth and bedrock belief that our rights are derived, not from government, but from God. Married for nearly five decades to his lovely bride, Lynda, the proud father of four and grandfather of six, Don Wildmon's life is a testament to faith, family and freedom. In recognition of all his achievements and those yet to come, The Family Research Council bestows upon Don the James C. Dobson fourth annual Vision and Leadership Award, given in the city of Washington, D. C. this 18th day of September in the year of our Lord 2010."

It had been a once-in-a-lifetime experience, never to be forgotten.

7

The Gala, I enjoyed it all

BY ALLEN WILDMON

The highlight of my work with the American Family Association came after I retired. Mickey, my wife, Lynn, my daughter, my sister Louise, her son Michael, his daughter Sara Beth and I attended the Faith, Family and Freedom Gala Dinner on September 18, 2010 in Washington, D.C. The dinner is a part of the "Value Voters Summit." This is when the conservative organizations get together each year, share ideas and listen to speakers aspiring to run for the presidency of America. As a part of the program, about two thousand of Don's peers from conservative organizations across the entire nation were there also to honor him. I remember watching the big TV screen while lying on the bed in our room at the Sheraton Hotel. An announcement written in big blue letters, surrounded by a red screen, and bordered on the edges by a black TV set flashed on the screen. The framed message for the viewer occupied the entire screen.

The message read:

6:00 PM – 7:00 PM
DIPLOMAT BALLROOM
RECEPTION WITH DON WILDMON

The message could be seen in every room and the lobby of the large hotel. I thought back to the time many years earlier when the American Family Association was first formed. One night Larry Durham, Don, and I had walked the grounds around the capitol at night. We walked past the lights casting their bright beams covering the capitol dome and not far from the huge Lincoln Memorial Reflection Pool. Don was in town to address the National Religious Broadcasters' Convention.

He was not on the program, but since national interest in his efforts had grown, he had asked for a few minutes to address the broadcasters. Don waited for two days, but no spot could be found.

Almost a same story happened 71-years prior to that date on April 9, 1939 when singer Marian Anderson was 42 and she sang her legendary open-air concert at the Lincoln Memorial. Anderson was a famous contralto of the day, and the concert was arranged after the Daughters of the American Revolution refused to let her perform at Constitution Hall because she was Black. An open air concert was arranged for her on the steps of the Lincoln Memorial on Easter Sunday. She sang to a crowd of more than 75,000 people lining the sides of the rectangle shaped pool. She later sang to the president in the White House.

I remembered thinking as I walked around the pool with bright reflections of the Lincoln Memorial bouncing up from it, "I wonder if Don's new organization would ever have any effect on the body which gathered nearby to govern the United States of America." After waiting for two days for the call for Don to speak to the convention (they were trying to squeeze him in), the call didn't come. Don, his brother-in-law Larry Durham and I headed home.

Don invited to speak at NRB

Don, a year later, was invited back to speak to the National Religious Broadcasters Convention. When he finished addressing the group, he received a standing ovation for several minutes.

I remember when Don's name was first brought up on the U. S. House of Representatives' floor and the floor of the U. S. Senate in 1989. Because of Don, both the Senate and the House were discussing the efforts of the man from Tupelo. He had stirred up a hornet's nest about taxpayer funding for the National Endowment for the Arts. He and Lynda were later invited to attend three presidential inaugurations.

That evening, after dinner, a voice came over the sound system: "Ladies and gentlemen, would you turn your attention to the screens now, for a video tribute to Don Wildmon."

A scene opened with Don turning the latch to a silver wire mesh gate leading to a little league baseball field. After he closed the gate, Don looked at the camera and said, "I think every little boy dreams of adventure; getting the bad guy fighting the battle, and slaying the dragon. That's the best part!" Don laughs and continues as the camera does a close-up of Don slowly walking across the green baseball field with a brown dirt-shaped diamond in the middle of the field. He was wearing his soft black shoes, brown pants and walking with the assistance of his black walking cane.

"We're born with a desire to take on the world; and the desire to be a part of something bigger than ourselves." Don said as the camera moves from a shot of a brown home plate to Don sitting on the little league players' bench in the dugout. Holding his walking cane in hand, he looks up at the camera and says, "A desire to win the game. That's the best part."

The camera switches to a young boy sitting in the dugout wearing a maroon ball cap with a pronounced white capital 'T' imprinted above the bill. He looks depressed as a fellow teammate has just struck out at bat. The coach, looking at the disheartened young player then says in a strong voice, "Hey! … You're up!"

Then Don's voice returns and he says, "But not every bad guy gets caught. And not every monster is slain." The camera shows the young player leaving the bench wearing a maroon ball shirt with 'Thunder' written on it. Don's voice continues as he says, "Sometimes the score just isn't in our favor."

The video shows the young player returning from striking out, cap removed and looking even more dejected when the camera returns to the coach's face and the coach says in a soft voice while almost eyeball to eyeball to the young player as the coach questions, "Hey, do you still think this game's possible to win?" The young player, hesitating, then in a dejected voice looks at the coach, and says, "I guess."

Then the coach says to the young player in a stronger voice, "Well, do you think this game's worth winning?" The young player then shakes his head up and down to signal his agreement with the coach. And the coach asks, "Then how should you play?" The young man smiles and answers in a firm voice, "To win." The coach, half of his face shaded by the bill of his ball cap and looking at the young player with a wide smile on his face says, "That's right!"

The next scene shows the young player placing a worn black baseball helmet on his head. The camera pans to one of Don's black shoes as he is shown walking toward a green bag lying against the wall in the dugout holding the bats belonging to the team. He reaches down, takes a grip on a blonde wooden bat, and says, "Today there is an ongoing battle in America," as the young player is shown with hope in his eyes at home plate ready to bat. Don continues, "It is a battle for our culture." The camera switches to the catcher of the opposing team wearing a black catcher's face mask and squatting with the brown catcher's mitt held high as the small white ball with the red stitches comes whizzing by the batter and makes a dull thumping sound as it hits the pocket of his leather mitt.

The camera switches to various intermittent color scenes of strip clubs, neon lighted porn video store fronts, drug filled streets, a gay (homosexual) bar, neon beer signs and prostitutes walking the streets looking for customers.

Don's voice can be heard:

"We have to fight for our freedom!" Don says as a scene of African Americans are shown marching across the Edmund Pettus Bridge in Selma, Alabama, in 1965 while exercising their rights to participate in our nation as full red-blooded Americans, born on American soil.

Don continues, (then fight for) "Our families, – a scene of a woman's white-gloved hand is seen reaching for a man's hand (with green-stemmed red roses in the background) in a marriage ceremony – and fight for our marriages and our country.

A camera shot of green, orange and red cocktail glasses sitting on a bar occupy the video screen. Don can be heard off-screen, "Our battle is not against flesh and blood, congress, Hollywood, the media or the entainment industry." A camera shows a red-lettered rectangle sign on a white background which states "Must be 21 to enter" – our battle is a war that can only be won in the hearts of man." The camera switches back to Don in his dark red sports shirt sitting on the little league ball field bench and then changes to a close up face shot of the young player wearing the maroon baseball cap with his bat held high with an unwavering look on his face; ready to take a full swing at the ball.

The next shot is the coach shaking his head "yes" as the umpire calls another strike on the young player at bat. The scene of a white sign on a background of black is shown stating, "Adult". The camera shows Don shaking his head "yes" and then a shot of the young man holding the bat looks at Don and shakes his head "yes." The loud cracking sound of a solid wood bat meeting the cow-hide leather skin baseball is heard. Don's questioning voice is heard to say, "How are you gonna play?"

Don is shown facing the camera saying, "For more than thirty years, I have been involved in the cultural wars. We fought many battles, (said with a chuckle) some of 'em we lost, but we fought 'em and we intend to go on fighting because the war has not been won. The war is not over yet."

Don is shown with his black walking cane lying in his lap and he is unconsciously rolling it back and forth slightly with both of his brown aged spotted hands. "My appeal to you is to get involved, to get in the game, to pick up the bat, and … who knows, you may get a single, you might get a double, and every now and then, you may even hit a home run! So I urge you … plead with you … to get involved. What's at stake? The future of our children, and our grandchildren. Western Civilization as we have known it for two thousand years. Let me say it again, what's at stake here, Western Civilization as we have known it for 2000 years.

"There are those who want to remove Christ from our society, that's the reason we've got to get in the game, and stay in the game. I don't know what you're gonna do; I hope you will stay in the game, but as for me, I'm gonna fight, I'm gonna play … play to win. And I hope you will too!"

The video ended with Don passing the bat to Tim and saying, "You're up."

After the video, Master of Ceremonies Tony Perkins called to Don and Lynda. "Don and Lynda, before you come to receive the James C. Dobson Vision Leadership Award, I want to share personally with you. Don, you have served with humility and you show the scriptures to be true because 'To the one who gives, it will be given back to him,' and as Dick Bott, earlier in the evening said, 'I have never seen Don Wildmon with a closed hand. I've always seen him with his hand open, willing to give whatever he has, to further the movement, to further the cause, to help someone else.'"

With stairs leading to a raised stage and with a spotlight beamed on the podium, Mickey and I watched from our seats at our table as a man of courage who had dared to speak out against the direction of America's moral compass, rose from his seat.

Don looked tired

We could tell he was worn-out and weary from fighting the good fight for thirty-three years for change in America. Also, he had been at death's door just a few months before while spending four months in hospitals. A mosquito had bitten him and caused St. Louis encephalitis. With his wife Lynda, by his side, Don left his table as his children and grandchildren looked on from the crowd below the stage. He held his black walking cane in his right hand and walked with a halting limp toward the stage. Neal Clement, Don's son-in-law, and Larry Durham,

Don's brother-in-law, and fellow worker from the American Family Association, left their seats and were following close behind in case he fell while climbing the steps to reach the stage podium.

Tears flowed down mine and Mickey's face, along with others in the crowd as we watched the scene unfold while those in the audience gave him a thundering applause. I looked back over the years and remembered the ridicule, accusations made, and the many daily "rocks" and name calling from the secular world which were thrown his way. Mockery had been made and ridicule revealed from many fellow Christians and from those who had surrendered their souls to the siren call of the world's modern ways. He had stood tall during the past thirty odd years, and he never gave up or gave in. He and his family had paid a price for fighting on the field of battle for Biblical values. Fighting for what was right in spite of the hate-spewed words of the crowd of those opposing him.

I remembered the day when Don asked me to research the law and see if America's motto, In God We Trust, was law. It was indeed national law, and because of him "America's Motto Posters" now hang on every schoolroom wall in the state of Mississippi and other schoolroom walls and businesses throughout the nation.

When Don and Lynda reached the podium, Tony presented the award.

Don said a few words from his podium view overlooking the audience, which included pointing out a colleague.

Don recognizes a long time warrior

Phyllis Shaffley was in the crowd and he thanked her for the many years of service in her fight on the battlefield of the cultural war. This was typical Don, recognizing other's achievements.

The hundreds of attendees rose to their feet and gave her a resounding applause when he pointed her out in the crowd from his red, white, and blue, half-moon circular podium.

OneNewsNow (the in-house news organization which Don founded) reported comments made by other Christian leaders who didn't speak from the platform podium, but were interviewed separately. The following are comments of some of those interviewed:

Greg Quinlan with Parents and Friends of Ex-Gays who has worked with the American Family Association since 1992 was one of the first to be interviewed. "Wildmon's organization" he shared, has been, "a blessing to our ministry and to the culture at large.

"But for the most part, I'd like to thank Don Wildmon and AFA (for) is this: you've come alongside us when others would not," said Quinlan. "You fought the battle with us to stop the homosexual agenda in every way we can. You've been there as a resource, you've been there as a foundation, as a place for us to stand and build on – and for that, we could not possibly have done what we have done."

Ex-gays, argues Quinlan, prove that change is possible; that homosexuality does not have to last a lifetime. "And that message has gotten out in a large part because of Don Wildmon and the AFA – and for that, I just want to say thank you very much," he said.

Another long time warrior has kind remarks for Don

Bill Johnson with the American Decency Association (ADA) was the first named State Director for the American Family Association in the late 1980s. That affiliated group eventually spun off to become the American Decency Association. "Wildmon," he says, "Is truly the real deal." Asked to describe Wildmon with one word or phrase, Johnson thoughtfully replied – Prophet."

"Don Wildmon (as a visionary) was seeing 10 to 15 years ahead of most of us. What you see is what you get with Don," Johnson continued. "It's hard to say it in just simply one word, but he's truly the real deal; the most exceptional man I've ever met in my life. With Don Wildmon you always felt like you were really speaking with a Godly man. I think American Family Association is going to go on for many, many years because it is built upon the right stuff."

Don Wildmon had become a household name and had earned the respect of millions throughout the nation despite the secularist attacks on him. The public had learned the truth about his courage to speak out in spite of the secularists' contempt for him. He had reversed the elite media-made opinion of him throughout the Christian community (although none would admit it). He was no longer the "red-neck" preacher from Mississippi, but a man of courage, character and respect.

Don jokes about the mosquito bite

During his short talk, while sometimes leaning against the podium, he made the crowd laugh with a joke about a "conservative mosquito" which had bitten and hospitalized him for four months as he lay near death's door the previous year.

He said, "It must have been a liberal mosquito. How did I know it was liberal? Because when I went on all the TV talk shows they would always say, 'We've got to have somebody from the other side, we've got to have somebody who is neutral, and we have got to have a host.' Now that's three liberals to one conservative. If you can't whip three liberals, you're not a conservative.'" The room was filled with laughter.

A fellow Christian traveler in the cultural war had written a song especially for Don for the occasion, and the audience's attention focused on Eric Horner as he sang, *In God We Trust.*

Over the years, he had not surrendered to the public's call or to the secular humanist ways, nor the liberal left's attempt to remove the meaning of the Cross from American society and never would surrender in his fight against America's anti-Christian elite, even until his last breath is drawn.

His position had been distorted from the beginning of the organization in 1977 by others mentioned in the preface of this book and because he is a Christian. Each comment of hate toward him is a compliment, reflects a mark of his success, and is a reminder of his accomplishments in life. God forgives those who hate. The Cross is still there for those who have followed life's "perverted" path. We have all sinned.

And when Don had finished with his few words from the stage platform, the crowd again rose to their feet and gave him an exceedingly long standing ovation as he exited the stage's descending steps, while leaning on Lynda and his black walking cane. The son of a Christian father and mother who taught their children to do their very best to live by The Golden Rule had made his mark on the nation. I was proud to be called his brother.

SECTION THREE
Getting the Word Out

8

Building a radio network of nearly 200 stations

One of the things I had to do, in the battle for traditional values, was to learn to deal with the media. I would often give an interview with a reporter, but when the reporter's story appeared, I hardly recognized who the reporter was writing about. One of the magazines which I read weekly was *Broadcasting*. It was a trade publication dealing with the various aspects of broadcasting.

In the fall of 1989 a very short story appeared in *Broadcasting* which told of a change at the Federal Communication Commission. The FCC had just opened a new way of delivering the signal of FM radio stations. The FCC voted to allow FM stations to deliver their signal by satellite.

For years I had been interested in radio. Earlier I was asked to become a part of a group which was seeking to buy a small AM station in Tupelo. I had to decline because I did not have the money.

The FCC rule change allowed translators to be fed by satellite. A translator is a small, low power station with a range of 12-15 miles and requires no personnel at the translator transmitting site. The cost to build a translator station was about $15,000. I immediately saw the possibilities. But there was a catch. You can't feed translators with a signal if there is no FM station to send the signal.

I had saved $3,000,000 waiting for the Lord to tell me where to invest it. I often said you should not spend money simply because you have it. I had a standing rule: You don't spend money which you don't have. Another rule of mine: You don't borrow money. AFA has borrowed money only one time since it began in 1977. That money was borrowed to help pay for the cost of constructing the first building. My way of budgeting was to always spend less than you take in.

With money in the bank and an idea that could put unmanned FM radio transmitter stations in small communities across the country, I decided it was time to act. I hired a person to prepare the application for AFA. On December 6, 1989, the first AFA application was submitted to the FCC. Now all AFA had to do was to wait for approval. But others did not want AFA to get a license to broadcast.

MPB opposed AFA efforts to build a radio station

The Mississippi Public Broadcasting wrote the FCC asking the commission to deny AFA's application for a station. MPB didn't want to build a station. They just didn't want AFA to be allowed to build a station. This despite the fact MPB had more than a dozen stations with signals which covered the entire state. Furthermore, MPB said AFA was asking for too much power. AFA had filed for a 50,000 watt station. MPB said that was too much power for AFA to have. But MPB had nearly a dozen stations with 100,000 watts. MPB went on to argue that AFA should not be granted a license because some other station might want to increase their power in the future and AFA's station might interfere with that station.

I learned it took the FCC about six months to approve an application. Since AFA had filed on December 6, 1989, it should hear from the FCC sometime around June of 1990. So I waited. And waited. June 1990 came and went. No word from the FCC. Finally, after the application had been in the hands of the FCC for nearly a year, I called my U.S. Senator and asked for help. The senator contacted the FCC and asked about the AFA application. The FCC assured the senator the agency was working on the application. Then, on February 20, 1991, the FCC granted permission for the AFA to build their station. On August 21, 1991, AFR went on the air. It was an exciting day at AFA when AFR went live.

I remember calling all the staff to the small room where the uplink equipment was located and listening to the station's signal going up to satellite and back down to the receiving station. That was 25,000 miles one way. It was quite an experience for a group of homegrown engineers and broadcasters. AFA had taken a giant step forward. AFA could begin building the network of small translator stations of which I had dreamed back in the fall of 1989.

First translator to go on air was in Jackson, Tennessee

The first translator to go on the air was in Jackson, Tennessee. I remember the time I drove the 100 plus miles from Tupelo to Jackson to listen to the station. I drove around Jackson listening to the signal, pinching myself to make sure the signal was real, that AFA actually built a translator station, that a signal going out from the main studios in Tupelo could be heard miles away.

I do not remember the order in which the stations went on the air. I do remember on one day, the AFA engineers turned on three stations. It was possible to do because every thing had been prepared. The tower and antenna were ready. Electricity had been turned on. The building and air conditioning was complete. All the engineers had to do was to place the small transmitter in the control rack and turn on the power.

When I began my dream of small radio stations across the country, I set a goal of 500 stations. I might have achieved that number had not the FCC changed the rules. As AFR began to grow, others became interested in the concept. Soon they began filing on top of AFA's applications, meaning they filed for the same location where AFA had filed. Some even simply copied AFA applications, changed the name and submitted the application as their own. In order to achieve my goal of 500 stations, I set up an assembly line to file for permits. About five people were in the line, each with their respective duties. It was a cost effective way to operate. To job out the preparation of applications to another party would have cost $3,000 each.

We need you to withdraw your application so we can get it

I even had many who wanted to build a Christian station call and ask me to withdraw AFA's application so they could get the station. I did withdraw several applications, but those who wanted a Christian station did not get the permit to build a station. The Public Broadcasting Service stations nearly always got the permit. All of AFA's withdrawing didn't help the local Christian group, it only hurt AFA. AFA's efforts to build a national network of Christian stations got plenty of criticism from other Christian stations. Two national Christian programs even pulled their programs from American Family Radio stations. Years later, many Christian broadcasters appreciated AFA's efforts. And those who had pulled their programs asked AFA to put them back on AFR. And we did.

I saw my dreams of a 500 station network come to an end. My idea of a national network was ended by a ruling from the FCC. There were so many applications filed for stations that the FCC made a new ruling, changing horses in the middle of the stream. The new method of deciding who would get a permit to build a contested station was weighted in favor of the National Public Radio and Corporation for Public Broadcasting folks. If there was an NPR/CPB type application, they would get the permit. If it boiled down to just Christian applications, the FCC granted the weakest application. This was done to cut down on the influence of Christian stations. Because of the changes at the FCC, AFA lost about 200 applications. AFA did end up with about 190 stations.

In addition, because there were so many groups who were influenced to build a station in their community, America ended up getting about 200 new Christian stations. They were not AFA stations. They were independent Christian stations.

Cow scratches her back, station goes off the air

We have had some entertaining situations at American Family Radio. In one case we had a $50,000 transmitter go off the air. When the engineers got to the transmitter site, they searched high and low for the problem. After spending much more time than usual on the problem, they finally found what was wrong. A roach got caught inside the transmitter causing it to throw a fuse. Many of our transmitter sites were located in rural areas.

In another case, one of our receiving dishes kept getting knocked off frequency. We checked everything we knew which could cause the problem. Finally, nearly giving up, we saw the problem clearly. A cow was scratching her back on the receiving dish. We solved that problem by mounting the dish on top of the equipment building.

In another situation, a station went off the air. When the engineers got to the site, they discovered the coax cable had been eaten in half by a goat. The coax cable is what carries the signal from the transmitter to the antenna on top of the tower. It cost about $45 a foot. It is made of copper tubing covered with a coating of tar.

Today American Family Radio is doing what it was envisioned to do, giving its audience the information and inspiration to be a good citizen and an informed Christian.

9
AFR News fills the vacuum
for radio news

As I was building the AFR network, I knew there was a great need for a news organization to go along with the other information AFA was providing. As a first move toward a news network, AFR did begin one minute of news at the top of the hour. While it wasn't much, it was a beginning. As months passed, it became apparent AFR should move more into the news.

The listening audience wasn't getting any news on the issues of importance to AFA/AFR from the secular outlets. Gradually the news staff grew. Finally, I figured it was time to make the leap to a full time news staff. I knew AFR needed someone with experience to head up the news division.

One day I received a call from Fred Jackson, who had years of experience with the Canadian Broadcasting Corporation. Fred was inquiring about an opening on the AFR news team. Fred had two reasons for wanting to work at AFR. First, he was tired of working for a liberal news organization, and second, his wife was from Mississippi, about a two hour drive from AFR's studios.

What AFR is offering isn't news

Anyone who listened could tell the secular news media in the United States was biased against the conservative movement and favorable toward the liberal position. Nothing of a religious matter short of the Pope coming to America made the news. And when the news did cover religious matters, it was nearly always in a negative light. When AFR began covering events and issues from a Christian perspective, it was refreshingly different. One listener called the network to tell us "what AFR was airing wasn't news because it contained references to Christian activities."

I said there were probably thousands of listeners who felt the same way. Those listeners had become so familiar with the bias they couldn't recognize the bias. The secular media has been very successful in shaping the views of many Americans. With time, God showed me that to get my message out, I would have to create our own news outlet. The old saying was this: "There is freedom of the press, if you own the press."

Various circumstances came together which resulted in a meeting between Fred and me at the network headquarters in Tupelo. Fred had spent nearly 20 years working for the radio news division of Canada's public broadcaster, the Canadian Broadcasting Corporation, or CBC. While working for such a major world network proved very beneficial from a journalistic training point of view, it became very clear to Fred in the mid-1990s that the CBC was quickly developing a new attitude towards news journalism. Instead of simply focusing on the facts, the news division leaders wanted more "point of view" journalism and by that they meant a liberal slant on the major issues of the day.

A news person from Canada comes to the states

A Canadian by birth, Fred knew that in the U.S. he could go as far as his talent and drive could take him. Fred had a message and he wanted to get it out. The message? Here are his words. "There are values that have made the United States the greatest nation in the world. Those values, based on Scripture, have allowed this country to prosper and grow and have made it the envy of other nations. And it is those scriptural values of freedom and opportunity to use your God-given abilities that have driven millions from other parts of the world to seek the United States as their new home."

And so through prayer and contacts, Fred found himself in October 1996 sitting across a desk from me in my office in Tupelo discussing the possibility of his coming to AFR as news director.

Fred accepted the job offer and six months later, after completing all the appropriate immigration paperwork and moving his family to Tupelo, he began to work out his calling at AFR. It was his goal to create a professional news service that would educate the audience and motivate people to get involved in the fight to save those God-ordained values.

According to Fred, the action plan was simple. Expose our listeners to the developments of the day and let them hear how Christian leaders were responding. As our staff numbers grew, we were able to increase the number of daily newscasts and to cover more of the issues our listeners needed to hear.

At first, it was difficult to find enough stories to fill the daily newscasts. That didn't last long. The secular crowd became very aggressive in their efforts to undermine Christian values. That gave AFR News plenty to report. Fred began to assign areas to particular reporters to monitor within this spiritual battle.

He assigned reporters to cover the daily agenda of policy initiatives in Washington. We also soon realized our nation's school system was becoming an incubator for the secular left, inserting their propaganda into the minds of the nation's young people. And sadly, we increasingly had to alert people to what was happening in the country's major denominations. We found ourselves covering an evolution of confusion in many denominations, particularly in the area of accepting homosexuality. Activist homosexuals were not only welcomed; they soon were welcomed in the pulpit.

In recent years, AFR News has expanded our coverage to include Christian perspectives on the country's economic problems and examining the impact of our society growing more accepting of Islam, despite the fact most of the world's terrorist incidents are carried out by Muslims in the name of their religion.

Tracking the anti-Christian bias

A further trend American Family News has been able to track is the growing open hostility towards those who simply want to live out their Christian faith. We have seen young people in our schools and colleges told they cannot speak about their biblical convictions because their words might offend others. Companies run by Christians have been told they cannot refuse to do business with activist homosexuals, even when their activities are contrary to Christian values.

Funding AFR news was not a cheap venture. I estimate it takes AFA about three quarters of a million dollars a year to keep the news division going. But God has been good to AFR and the money needed to support the news division is donated. Under Fred's supervision and working with a dedicated team, American Family News is now a professional news organization.

Thanks to what AFR is doing, I believe AFR is finally convincing people the spiritual warfare we have been talking about for years is real. And, I believe, this realization is prompting more people to get involved in the fight to return the country to the Christian values on which it was based.

10

Give them news they need

In the early 1990s I sought to expand the influence of AFR by creating our own news-gathering team for broadcast on AFR. I wanted to provide news reported from a Christian worldview and without the veiled liberal bias found in the secular news media.

While that effort was quite successful, it had limited exposure. AFR news was heard only a few minutes a day and only across its own stations. However, with the exploding popularity of the Internet as a news medium, I saw an opportunity in early 2000 for worldwide exposure of the news being reported by the AFR news team.

The objective behind this approach was quite simple: get "double duty" out of the original radio scripts being generated each day by the dedicated team of news reporters for American Family News by presenting those scripts in written form on the worldwide web. To facilitate that objective, a news editor was hired and space was made available on the AFA website for a few selected news pieces which would be updated every weekday. Within a few short weeks following this launch, I began to have a larger vision. Create a news service that would make copyrighted news reports available to other ministry websites as well as to Christian publications across the U.S. Thus, AgapePress was launched..

Using its own database of Christian newspapers and editors nationwide, the American Family Association introduced AgapePress to the public in late 2000. The copyrighted material, which was to be delivered via email every weekday, was made available free of charge to non-profit operations (and to churches as well for their use in newsletters and bulletins); and made available for a minimal subscription fee to for-profit operations (e.g., newspapers). The first response came from Warren Smith, the editor of the Charlotte World, who wrote: "Great idea! I only wish I'd thought of it first!"

AgapePress eventually launched its own website, providing its unique offering of AgapePress original news copy for upwards of 40-50 Christian newspapers and several hundred churches in America.

AFA periodically received testimonials from pastors reporting the material from AgapePress either made it into their sermons or acted as a catalyst for sermons. And the AgapePress website developed its own following of dedicated readers and its own stable of contributing columnists.

AgapePress also began sending a daily email to a mailing list of individuals around the country who wished to receive news from a Christian perspective in their computer mail box.

In 2007, AgapePress was absorbed into the American Family News department. The online news presence was given the name OneNewsNow.com. With a new emphasis on wanting to be the one place where Christians could get all their news, AFA signed a contract with Associated Press that allowed news from several arenas to be displayed at the new website. This allowed world news, political news, business news, and even sports from AP to be accessed by visitors to OneNewsNow.com. Missions related news from Mission Network News was also added.

The expanded, newly designed website for OneNewsNow allowed the addition of several syndicated conservative columnists, editorial cartoons, daily polls, and featured columns from ministries such as Answers in Genesis, Dave Ramsey, and Dr. Michael Youssef; all of which have worked together to grow online traffic to as high as 2.5 million page views/month as measured by Quantcast.com.

OneNewsNow.com, because of its affiliation with the established American Family Association and its credibility as a professional news gathering and reporting organization became a regular stop for numerous conservative and Christian news watchers and commentators that cites its reports.

In late summer 2012, in its effort to remain one of the top websites-of-choice for conservative evangelical Christians, OneNewsNow unveiled a newly designed website incorporating more graphics and Associated Press news images, as well as updated technology for its content management system.

OneNewsNow.com continues to send an email summary every day to an opt-in list of more than 700,000 individuals.

11

The AFA Journal has come a long way

When we started down this road in early 1977, I knew the U.S. Post Office was going to be my key to finding others who felt like I did about television programs, but with no real budget, it was a challenge. My first letter went to just a few hundred friends, family and acquaintances who I thought might be interested. We got it printed out, and Lynda and I sat down with the kids and hand-addressed them and put stamps on them. We didn't get a bulk mail permit – probably didn't qualify for one – until later that year after we established our non-profit status.

Our second newsletter, if that's what you'd call it, was a tri-fold 8.5" x 11" piece that we again hand addressed and stamped. It was postmarked April 27, 1977. The only copy I'm aware of that still exists is the one in our files. In my own personal scrawl, it is addressed to Mr. and Mrs. Ellis Wildmon – Mama and Daddy – at their Ripley, Mississippi, home. The headline on this one said, "Nationwide Turn Off The Television Week Scheduled July 24-30."

I had already surrendered to the fact that this was not going to be a short-term project; God was calling me to carry this issue farther, and I was confident He wanted me to go forward in an organized manner. I also had determined the name of the organization, so I called this second mail-out *The Newsletter of the National Federation for Decency*, which later became AFA. In it, I urged people to start local chapters of NFD. It also reported results of our very first study of sexual content and profanity on prime-time television, covering the period from January 30 to February 5.

From the outset, I counted on the content itself to capture the attention of readers; I didn't have the time or the expertise to work on making a layout appealing or finding great photos to illustrate the stories. The words would have to do it. That is a practice we pretty well followed until recent years.

Even small quantities of those early mail-outs were expensive, so I was excited to acquire an old offset press (with my own money) and set up a print shop on our dining room table. Boy, did I think I was in business! That old press served me well for a few years, but as our numbers grew, we outgrew the old press, too.

Early on, I had changed the newsletter format to a newspaper tabloid size page, and printed it on newsprint – giving readers lots of little black smudges on their fingers as they read. In November 1980, I began calling it *NFD Informer*. I realized its value, and I knew it needed to improve, but there was just not much way to make it a priority in those first few years. I still didn't have finances for the staff I needed. On top of that, speaking opportunities increased, and our mailing list was growing fast.

Somewhere along the way, the printing and mailing became too big a job for me, so we began using a newspaper printer in Kosciusko, Mississippi. He both printed and mailed for us, so that freed up a lot of my time for other needs in the ministry. In early 1983, I had a staff of six, but they had full days in administration, travel and speaking, data processing and bookkeeping. I began to think maybe it was time to hire an editor, so I put a small item on the front page of the May newsletter.

I asked for applicants who were "fully qualified and experienced in journalistic writing, design and layout, and advertising." Well, you probably know how God's plans are not always our plans. Such was the case this time. Several of the applicants I interviewed did, indeed, have the credentials I thought I required. Ironically, I wound up hiring a high school English teacher. He called and asked for an interview, and for some reason, I felt I needed to talk to him about the job. He didn't meet all the criteria, but he had the heart for ministry, so he became the full-time editor of the newsletter, and he's still at the post.

Over the years, we continued to try to make improvements as finances allowed. In October 1983, we abandoned the tabloid format and adopted a magazine-size page, still printing on newsprint, and still carrying very few graphics or artwork. At the same time we changed the name to *NFD Journal*.

Two improvements came in the mid 1980s, the first when we quit using the inky newsprint and opted for a heavier matte paper that made the text easier to read. In 1986, we changed papers again – to a slick finish paper. The next notable update was a simple reflection of the organization's name change to American Family Association at the end of 1987. Thus we arrived at the current name, *AFA Journal.* But we have continued to look for ways to improve the Journal's appearance and content.

In May 2011, we again updated the paper to a heavier matte finish that finally gives the *Journal* the feel and look of a magazine. No longer do we have to fold it for it to be sturdy enough to mail.

Some of the updates have required that we change printing companies, but that's not the only reason we've left one printing company for another. Trying to be responsible stewards of our resources in every way, we keep up with what other publications our printer may be printing. Many years ago, for example, we had a great working relationship with a printing company in a city not too far from our headquarters in Tupelo. We loved working with them, but the company was purchased by a larger printing operation that also printed one of the leading men's porn magazines. There was no question about it. We couldn't stay there, even though the company did excellent work. But we had to search for a new printer.

Another time, we left a printing company we'd worked with for 15 years or more because we received a bid from our current printer, and they could do our job much cheaper. We'd been with the other company so long that the account representative who called on us had become a personal friend. But we had to go, because we are responsible to God to use our resources frugally.

Our latest effort to make the *Journal* more effective in its impact for our readers came at the beginning of 2012 when we redesigned both the cover and the inside pages, adding richer, deeper color and making use of many more graphics. At the same time, we began increasing the number of pages in almost every issue. So, even as we have more appealing photos, charts and graphic elements, content has not suffered.

Five full-time staff members produce 11 issues of the *Journal* each year, but realistically, they all wear more than one hat at AFA. Still, they publish a magazine we can be proud of, issue after issue. In fact, today's *Journal* writers are winners of numerous national awards at Evangelical Press Association, regional awards at Southern Christian Writers Conference, and a variety of other recognitions.

The bottom line is two-pronged. First, we try to produce a quality product – a visually appealing magazine packed with relevant content for Christian families struggling to thrive in a society that is often hostile both to the institution of the family and to the Christian faith. Second, we try to do it the most economical way possible. When I look back at those early years when I was trying to do it all by myself, I never could have imagined a monthly AFA magazine of the quality we have today.

I give the credit to the *AFA Journal* staff. The *AFA Journal* is, indeed, a class product.

SECTION FOUR
Potpourri

12

How the old-line media treat Christians

If you want to change a culture, allow only your point of view to be promoted. I learned in my dealings with the networks and Hollywood. Television allows the viewer to go to places you would never go to in real life. And it makes sure their viewpoint is more reasonable than those with whom they disagree.

For instance, the vast majority of people have never been in a hospital operating room, but we know what goes on in the room because we have seen it on television several times. Not only that, but you can create an image of the doctors in that room. With television, one can make the doctors to be cruel, dumb, careless, or hateful. But you can also make the doctors to be compassionate, kind, smart, loving or understanding.

Did you ever notice that prostitutes are always presented in a sympathetic light? It is no surprise that many times the point is made that this is the only way a mother can make enough money to feed her baby. Why is this so? It is because those who are responsible for the entertainment feel sex outside marriage is no big deal, and if a woman wants to prostitute her body, it is her right to do so.

You could apply the same to homosexuals. The homosexual will always be presented in a positive light. Why? Because the overwhelming majority who make movies or report on homosexual issues are sympathetic to the homosexual agenda.

Let me ask you a question. Can you identify one program on the secular networks which depicts Christians in a positive light? By never showing a Christian family, or anyone going to church or anyone who lives out his faith – and this continues for some twenty-odd years, it most definitely has an effect on the behavior of the viewer. Not long ago there was a report that over half of church going teens drop out of the church scene when they go to college, and many of them never go back to the church.

This screening out of Christians probably began in the early sixties. Somewhere in the seventies or eighties, Christians started being shown in a negative manner. We should not be surprised. The anti-Christian movement controls nearly all the portals of influence – law, entertainment media, news media, etc.

Through their programs, those in media use their positions to present Christians as greedy, liars, murderers, cheats, hypocrites, etc. When nearly the only place a child sees Christians in action is the local church and home, it is not too surprising when they go to college and don't come back to church.

Perhaps the greatest gain the entertainment media has made in changing society (for their side) has been in changing society in the area of sexual behavior.

For nearly fifty years the entertainment media has put a sex scene (often more than one) in nearly every movie and program. Most of the time, the sex scene was not relevant to the plot. It was put in for one reason: to change the attitude of the public toward sex. I hate to admit it, but they have been very successful. Like the frog in the boiling kettle, this change was slipped into the entertainment so slowly and quietly society hardly knew it had happened.

Don't expect to see a fair and balanced portrayal of Christians from the old-line media outlets. Hopefully, more Christians and entertainment companies will move to combat the negative portrayal.

This is the message our children have grown up with: If it feels good, do it.

13

God came through with a miracle, then did it again

Once I knew what God wanted me to do with my life, I knew it would take money and money was one thing I did not have. I gave up my job as a minister in order to begin AFA. I knew I would have to raise about $50,000 in the next year to provide me with some income and to fund the activities of AFA.

One of the things I did was to ask a very good friend to keep the books for AFA. Actually, she didn't keep the books, rather she kept the book. You see, she only had one book to keep. That book was a very small 3x5 notebook with the inscription on the front cover: LEDGER. She listed the amount of income AFA took in and the amount paid out.

The first entry in the accounting ledger was a deposit of $392 dated August 5, 1977. The next four entries were to Postmaster for $65, $60, $21.59, and $6.85. The next entry was to South Central (phone) for $356.87. On August 14, 1978, she made a deposit of $408. It would be November 21 before there was a deposit of $1000 or more. The next deposit of more than $1000 was made on March 29, 1979. On June 14, 1979, a deposit of $1505 was made. And on February 3, 1980, AFA made our largest deposit to date, $2489. It had taken two and a half years to have a deposit of more than $2400.

I have often pointed out that about 90% of the donations to AFA are $25 or less. AFA has never had a host of large supporters. A handful of donors support AFA with donations of $100,000 or more. Many contributors made a real sacrifice with their giving. One elderly lady sent AFA a money order for $10. She said she was skipping her medicine in order to make the donation. I promptly wrote her thanking her for the gift and telling her AFA was returning her donation and for her to just pray for AFA.

No. I'm not in it for the money.

On one of the many trips I made, I preached at a church in Pensacola, Florida. After the sermon, I invited those present to come to the altar and pray about their involvement. After the service was over, a lady came up to me and said, "You know, you are the real thing. You are not in it for the money that is for sure." Rather stunned, I replied, "Why do you say that?" "Because when you knelt to pray at the altar, I saw the holes in your shoes," she responded.

No, I was not in it for the money. The first year out of seminary my salary was $4500, less than $100 per week. That also happened to be the exact amount which I owed on my seminary loans. It was a real struggle at times. Twice I had to go to my parents for money to pay our bills. I decided after going to my parents two times, I would find some way to earn enough money to pay the bills. I had some experience in writing and it came easy for me. Over the next several years I earned enough so we did not have to worry about how we spent every dollar.

I had some interesting situations concerning money as I tried to raise money to fund AFA. The ministry sends an "Action Letter" each month asking supporters to take a particular action. One supporter collected the letters for several months and sent them back to AFA with a note saying I had hired a professional fundraiser. I had not. There was also the implied threat he was going to stop his donations. I checked the computer and found he had given AFA $3000. Now, $3000 at that point in AFA history was a considerable amount of money. Surely I didn't want to lose such a good contributor.

I did something many professional fundraisers would never even think of doing. I thanked the supporter for his past gifts. But I also told him I was very disappointed that he had taken no action on any of the letters. Then, in a kind way, I told the supporter if all he could do was to send AFA money and ignore the request to take action, he should find another ministry to support. The gentleman remained a devout supporter for many years.

God sent His human messenger that Saturday

I am one who believes God moves in mysterious ways, as hymn writer William Cowper said. God has ordered the universe to function in a particular way. But every now and then God will move out of the ordinary to do something miraculous. This has happened to me a few times in my life. One of the times was in the fall of 1979. Conservatives held a large rally attended by thousands in Dallas. I wanted to go, but did not for two reasons. One was I didn't have the money, and the other was that I was already doing what was going to be the central core of the conservative movement.

On that Saturday, I worked in my office upstairs in my home. One of the things I did on that Saturday morning was to see how the finances stood. After I counted all the money AFA had, and subtracting what AFA owed, we were $5,000 in the hole. I did not have a clue on how I was going to get $5,000. I left my study and went outside to mow the yard. While mowing, Lynda came out and told me I had a phone call. Going to the phone, I asked Lynda who it was. She told me it was a person who owned a chain of stores.

The person on the other end made small talk for a minute or two. Then he told me he was in Dallas and asked why I wasn't there. I explained to him about the lack of money. "Well, we are out here meeting and you are staying home and doing something. I want to help you. Monday I'm sending you a check for $5,000," he said. Never in the conversation was it mentioned that AFA was $5,000 short. I believe that person was sent by God, doing something extraordinary.

God does it again

Do you want a repeat? Try this. I am working in my office. I have just figured out AFA is $5,000 in debt. What will I do? How will I pay the bills? After I completed assessing the finances, I turned to other duties. About two hours later the phone rang. I answered. The person calling identified himself and asked me if I remembered him. I had to tell him that I did not recognize the name. He then told me that about a month earlier he had sent AFA a check for $300. I immediately recognized him. At that time AFA did not get very many $300 gifts. He asked how things were going and we chatted for a little while. Then he told me he and his wife had just written AFA a check for $5,000 and they were putting it on the shelf until Monday, when they would put it in the mail.

In operating AFA, which has a budget that runs into the millions of dollars, I had one simple rule: Always spend less than what comes in. I followed that rule in building AFA.

AFA has borrowed money only one time since it's beginning in 1977. That was to purchase a plot of ground on which to build our offices. I borrowed $90,000 to purchase the lot. The loan was paid off in six months and AFA has never borrowed again. AFA owns all the land, buildings, and equipment it has. AFA does not owe one penny on anything. We are audited annually and are a member of the Evangelical Council of Financial Accountability.

14

Thank God, I failed the course

In May of 1953, I was selected to participate in all expense paid Boy Scout Junior Leadership Training course at Philmont Scout Ranch in New Mexico. The mission of JLT, as it was called, was to provide six weeks of intense training to help the scouts become future leaders. Thirty-two scouts from around the country were put together to form a troop. The scouts learned to live outdoors, to fulfill normal everyday duties, to assume responsibility, to be held accountable for their actions and to learn how to relate to each other. I did not know it when I began the six week training course, but it was an experience that would change the life of this Eagle Scout.

On the first day at Philmont, the scout leaders were teaching the scouts how to use an axe. The scouts were very interested and paid much attention during the exhibition. All, that is, except me. I was goofing off and having a good time. At the end of the presentation by the adult scout leaders, I was asked to show the other scouts the proper way to split a log. The leaders had noticed I wasn't paying attention and called on me for that very reason. But I was feeling comfortable to do the task easily enough. I proceeded to take the axe in hand, raise it up and then, with only one hand on the axe handle, let it fall.

The axe glanced off the log and cut into one of the new, thick, heavy- duty plow shoes I had bought to wear while at Philmont. The axe cut went about two inches into the boot. The axe blade cut the boot between the big toe and the next toe. If the axe had been a half-inch in either direction, I would have had a bloody boot and only four toes.

That experience did little in getting me to change my attitude. I didn't change. I just wanted to be the center of attention and a scout the other scouts found entertaining. Back at home I was friends with a couple of boys who were the center of attention. I saw all the attention they were getting and decided to follow their example.

I was helping another scout one morning and we were laughing and joking and playing around while putting a saddle on a donkey. The other scout's leg got tied up in some rope. I and the other scout were still laughing when the donkey started running, pulling the other scout behind him. It was a situation which could have ended in death for the other scout. Fortunately, the rope came loose before the donkey had gone very far. Other scouts heard us laughing and thought I was laughing at the scout entangled in the rope. I tried to explain why I was laughing, but the other scouts did not believe me. The incident would come back to haunt me when I prepared to go home.

I had a great time during those six weeks

Every morning each scout and his patrol were inspected to see if everything was in order as it should be. If there were duties left undone, or not properly done, the individuals and his patrol were given demerits.

I had a great time those six weeks. I played and worked alongside the other scouts, joked with them, and made many friends.

At the end of six weeks, the scouts prepared to go back to their homes. The night before the course ended, there was a big bonfire. The names of those who had passed the course were read and each then went to the front to receive his certificate. Since my name began with a W, I knew my name would be near the end. I listened as the last name was called. It suddenly dawned on me, I had failed! It was a crushing blow for this 15-year-old Eagle Scout. Someone had paid my way. Someone had driven over a thousand miles to get me to Philmont. The scout leaders had prepared the program to help me succeed in life. I let my fellow hometown scouts down.

What made it more difficult to take was the fact each of the members of Philmont JLT Troop 14 had done the voting. Those who knew me best had voted not to pass me. When asked why I and four others failed, I was told the other four did not meet the physical requirements, but I failed because of my attitude. As we left Philmont, I made a pledge to myself. Never again would I try to be the center of attention. I did not pass the course, but it helped me overcome many obstacles which lay in my future.

15

Donahue had me set up, but he didn't win

One of the leading television talk show hosts whose attention we drew was Phil Donahue. He was a pioneer in television talk. We got his attention when we allowed a group of mothers to use our name in a press release blasting Donahue because of the amount of sex on his daily show.

Following the press release, Donahue called and invited me to be a guest on his show. I accepted and a date was set for the appearance. One of the pluses of this invitation was I could bring my two young daughters with me. It was a real treat for them to get to make a trip like this. Normally the show was aired from his studios in Chicago. It so happened the day we were scheduled to be on the program they were telecasting from Salt Lake City. We flew out of Memphis with connections in Dallas. Donahue put us up in a very nice hotel.

After breakfast we got ready to go to the arena. When we arrived at the arena, we were taken to the green room. The green room is where guests and personalities were taken to have the make-up applied. Why it is called the green room I do not know. I don't know if I have ever been in a green room that was green.

While in the green room, waiting to have my make-up applied, I struck up a conversation with the lady who was applying the make-up. I asked if she traveled with the show when they were on the road. She told me she did. I asked her about her children, her spouse, where she grew up, etc.

We also talked about the show and all the entertainment greats who had been on the show. It was really a who's who in Hollywood. She showed me a list of those who would be on the program in the near fuure. I asked her if she knew what was the subject of the program for the next day. "Yes," she said, "it is about artificial insemination." I didn't think much about it. Just another sex oriented program. Phil Donahue made a good living talking about sex on his show.

For the next hour the girls and I sat in a section reserved for guests and VIPs. It happended Marlo Thomas, Donahue's wife, was present for the program. Everyone loved Marlo, the daughter of Danny Thomas. Donahue even introduced Marlo to the audience in an effort to win the favor of the audience. The show would be telecast from an arena which held approximately 10,000. Donahue intentionally put the stage I was to sit on in the middle of the arena. The arena was packed full. Not a seat was left.

When it came time for the show, I was sitting in the very center of the arena. The only light was the spotlight with its beam circling around me. It was so dark I could not see the audience.

Donahue revs up the crowd

Donahue spent one hour working the audience, telling them how beautiful the state of Utah was, how great the people in Utah were, what a great honor it was to broadcast his show from Utah.

I knew the program would be broken down into four segments. My strategy was to play it one segment at a time, to be respectful and to pray for God's help. I had a chair to sit in and a small table next to the chair. On the table was a glass of water. After I sat down, I leaned over and picked up the glass to get a drink. As I tried to pick up the glass, my hands were shaking so hard I could not hold the glass. I put the glass down and did not attempt to pick it up again.

But here is the interesting part. While outside I was as nervous as could be, inside I was as calm as I have ever been. I feel that was the

Holy Spirit. I may not be able to hold a glass of water, but I have no problem keeping a clear mind. I have never felt as secure as I did sitting in the middle of 10,000 people. Donahue's intent was to make me look dumb, stupid, narrow-minded, and a religious nut. You choose the rest.

Donahue opened the program with an introduction of me, trying to make me look foolish without making himself look opinionated. With all the preliminaries out of the way, Donahue opened up firing away. I can't remember what the questions were, but I remember they were questions I had heard hundreds of times. As we came down to the end of the first segment, I rated myself a passing grade. Donahue had not destroyed me. I felt good about how the first segment went. I had done no less than a tie. In in my opinion, a tie is a win for me. Donahue was the one who is supposed to win, since we were debating in his territory.

After the TV break, we returned and Donahue came at me again. I was cool and collected. He moved about in the audience, getting audience participation. What the viewing audience didn't know, nor nearly everyone in the arena didn't know, was from time to time Donahue would plant his people in the audience so he could go to them if things were beginning to get out of hand. And it was easy for him to get things back on track. That segment passed fast enough. I got through it without a big blunder. I rated myself at least a tie. As I said, a tie in my book was a win for me.

After another TV break and we were set again. Back Donahue came. I was more confident, more at ease. I'm relearning what I first learned a few years earlier: I have about as much sense as the famous people in the entertainment and news business. The third segment came to a close. The worst grade I gave myself was a tie. One more segment to go and then it would be over.

They ran the TV ads and then came back to Donahue. I sensed Donahue had given up on trying to make a fool of me. I think he was doing what I was doing: trying to end the debate before somebody slips and makes a fool of himself. Finally, the fourth segment ended and it appeared no one won the debate. While the cameras were playing the final ads, Donahue came over to me and said we have about 30 seconds left and asked was there anything I would like to say.

I told him no, and thanked him for asking. About that time, I suddenly remembered what the lady in the green room had said about tomorrow's program. Remember now, the microphone was still being used. Everyone was standing. Donahue had the microphone. "Give me your attention please. Rev. Wildmon has something to say." Donahue put the microphone in front of me. I asked Donahue what his show the next day was about.

Remember now, Donahue had been defending his program against those who said it contained too much sexual content. For one hour he had been saying his programs did not use much sexual content. His face suddenly turned red, the volume of his voice was real loud. He answered, "Our show tomorrow is about artificial insemination."

The crowd of 10,000 exploded with laughter. I had won the debate.

But the story doesn't end there. Two years later I was invited to be on his show again. This time I was one of three people forming a panel. I don't remember what the subject was or who were the other two guests. But I do remember going into the reception area to wait for someone to show us where to go.

As the lady in charge of the reception area came through the door, she looked at me and nearly screamed: "I remember you! You were on the show in Salt Lake City. We got more mail from that show than on any we have ever done."

I must have made an impression on her. Two years, one hundred and eight shows, and at least one hundred and eight guests later, she remembered me. Not bad for a country boy from Mississippi.

16

TV executive says you do not have the right to spend your money where you desire

In late August 1979 I accepted an invitation to appear on NBC's **Tomorrow Show** on September 13, in New York City. Tom Snyder was the host of the show. Snyder said he had to get someone from the other side to be on the program with me. Snyder selected Lee Rich, from Lorimar Productions, and producer of **Dallas** and **Helter Skelter**. NBC paid all the expenses for Allen and me and put us up in a first class hotel.

At times I could do reasonably well in debates because I had a distinctive advantage. I had debated the subject hundreds of times while my opponents usually had not debated the subject a single time. I was pretty good on my feet. The more pressure, the better I could get. And I carried notes that I could use if needed.

A few days prior to the show, I got a call indicating Rich had canceled his appearance due to some "arrangement problems." NBC rescheduled the program for a date prior to September 13. Rich canceled again. In fact, he cancelled a third time. He eventually agreed to appear. The reason he accepted the invitation was, I put a lot of pressure on him. I sent press releases to the media saying he was afraid to debate me, an ignorant country preacher from Mississippi. I sent out four such releases. I think he got tired of the press releases.

When we arrived at the NBC studio that afternoon we met Mr. Rich. He was accompanied by his wife. The debate started, and I got

Lee Rich's temper fired up pretty quickly. In the heat of the debate, Rich started shouting at me and the TV host. This wasn't supposed to be happening. The preacher from Tupelo wasn't supposed to have so many facts about TV. Even the host Tom Snyder was surprised I used proper grammar, even if it was with a Southern accent.

Rich is beginning to get angry

The more we went at it, the more angry Rich became. Snyder could not keep Rich quiet during commercial breaks. Let me share part of the conversation we had with Rich and Snyder. Snyder asked me: "The AFA goes after the advertisers of a program airing a lot of sex, violence, and profanity, why?"

I answered, "It's regrettable we've had to do this. But this was the only avenue left where our voice could really be heard.

"We learned early on the only language network executives seem to understand is money.

"Our philosophy is this: The advertiser's money is their money. And if an advertiser wants to spend their money on **Portrait of a Stripper**, which CBS is airing tonight, then they have that right.

"But we also believe our money is our money." I said, putting the emphasis on the word money.

Rich loses his cool

Rich replied, "Now, I believe Rev. Wildmon has the perfect right to say 'I'm not going to buy your product,' but, "not to threaten them (the advertisers)," and again he repeated, "Not to threaten them." Rich then started using the term "blackmail." Then a few sentences later, Rich reversed his prior statement and said, "Yes, but you don't have the right to spend your money any way you want." (Yes, that is what he said.) I knew I had him perplexed and on the "ropes" for his voice was getting louder and louder. I had him "down for the count."

A newspaper in New York had printed an interview with Rich a few weeks prior to the debate. The reporter quoted Rich as saying he was going to put as much sex and violence in the program **Dallas**, which he produced, as he could get away with. I ran across that quote weeks before, clipped it and carried it with me to the debate in my pocket.

While Rich was talking, I reached into my pocket and pulled out the article. "Here is an article from the New York Post in which…" Before I could finish my statement, Rich came screaming and yelling at me…"I am going to get away with as much sex and violence as I can."

Tom Snyder was visibly shaken. Turning to Rich, he said, "Lee, I came into this debate on your side. But now I find myself agreeing with Rev. Wildmon."

The debate was over and I won. Allen and I left and we could hear Rich shouting all the way to the elevator.

17

A bomb threat on our plane

One of the things Lynda and I both enjoy is traveling. My mother loved to travel, and she took two sons, ages eight and ten, with her on two trips. With one daughter having a baby in San Francisco and another in Newark, New Jersey, I got to take the train to both cities. The train ride to San Francisco was three days, and the train to Newark was two days.

In 1969 I saw an ad seeking tour hosts for a tour to Israel. I responded, did my homework, and found myself on the way to the Holy Land! Was I excited! It was my first time out of the country, other than a short trip to Mexico while a student in college. It was a really exciting trip for me. I must admit I was somewhat afraid of flying. I just used logic which showed plane travel is safer than automobile travel.

I remember the first morning in Jerusalem when I got up before daylight so I could see the sun rise over the Mount of Olives. And then we began the tour to all the places I had read about in the Bible: Jerusalem, the burial tomb, Bethlehem, Jericho, Dead Sea, Jordan River, Galilee, and on and on. All the others on the tour were moved like I was.

While it was my first trip to the Holy Land, it would not be my last. In fact, I toured Israel 20 more times. Counting my tours to Europe, I have crossed the North Atlantic 76 times, 38 times going and 38 times returning, spending a month out of my life in the air over the North Atlantic. The Israel Ministry of Tourism made me an honorary member of their Advisory Committee to the Ministry of Tourism in an effort to increase tourism.

On my tours, we would stop over at some country on the way home to make the tour more exciting. Over the years we visited Austria, Germany, Switzerland, Italy, Greece, France, Belgium and The Netherlands.

Plane warned of a bomb on board

As usual, some excitement was always nearby. Probably the most exciting, and certainly the most frightening event, involved Olympic Airlines. Olympic is the national airline of Greece. On our way home from Israel on one of our tours, we spent a couple of days in Greece visiting Athens and Corinth. Our flight home was about two hours late when we began boarding. After all were boarded, our plane was pushed back and taxied to the runway. We sat on the tarmac for another two hours. We were never informed what the problem was. The pilot hinted there was a problem with the electronics, but never explained.

Our flight to John F. Kennedy International Airport was smooth. No problem of any kind. But when we landed at JFK, it was anything but normal. Looking outside the plane we saw fire trucks and police cars with lights flashing. We were escorted to the most remote area of the airport. The plane's engines were shut down, but everyone's curiosity was going full blast.

We sat on the tarmac again for about two hours. Not one time while we were sitting on the plane were we given an explanation of any kind. All we knew was we were parked as far away from the terminals as we could get, and we were surrounded with fire trucks and police cars.

Finally we were told we would be departing the plane and we should leave in our seat any carry-on bags we had. We were told to leave the carry-on bags unlocked. So we lined up and filed out, one by one. Getting close to the terminal, we could see that media people filled the area. We were met by the media people. We learned from them there had been a bomb threat involving our plane.

When I learned about the bomb threat, I was much upset. We sat in the plane four hours, two in Athens and two in New York. If there had been a bomb, we would have been blown into eternity. The least they could have done was to get us off the plane. But no effort was made to remove us.

Then, to top it off, the locks on all the carry-ons were broken. Instead of simply pushing the lock to open, all our carry-ons were torn beyond repair.

I still haven't understood the logic of leaving the passengers on the plane for two hours. The supposed bomb would have been on the plane with us.

On another trip one lady lost her passport three times! I kid you not. Finally, I asked her to let me carry it for her. She had dropped it on the terminal floor, at the check-in desk and once in the restroom. I had to take another lady to the U.S. Embassy and spend a day getting a new passport.

On one trip I had a bus load with no empty seats. That made it easy for me because I did not have to count heads. I could simply see if there were any empty seats. Looking at the back of the bus and seeing all seats were filled, I told the driver all were accounted for and we could proceed toward the Sea of Galilee.

About an hour into our journey, a taxi pulled up alongside us and started blowing his horn. We pulled over to the side and here came one of the tour passengers. There was a mix up on seating on the bus and she was left behind. We set our departure time at 8 a.m. On the first day in the Holy Land we emphasized we would leave on time each morning so please do not be late for a day of touring. In fact, we did not leave our hotel until 8:15 on this day.

On another tour I had a passenger who talked back to an Israeli airport security officer. The officer departed with the passenger in tow. We emphasized you should just answer the questions. The rest of the tour members did exactly that. We were all on board the plane ready to be pushed back when we saw the passenger with the officer heading to the plane. The passenger boarded, and the door was shut. If you want to take a bet, I'll bet he will not talk back on his next trip. I had a personal friend go with us on one tour. After our time in the Holy Land, we had two days to tour Rome. The personal friend was an art teacher and the one thing she wanted to see was the Sistine Chapel.

Her tears turned to joy

Upon arriving in Rome and asking about the Sistine Chapel, we learned it was closed the next day and we would not be able to visit it. And it was too late in the day to see it on that day. It appeared my friend would not get to see the Sistine Chapel. She literally cried when told we would not get to see the chapel.

Since I had been doing business with the tour operator for several years, and had given him a lot of business, I called him. He was in Atlanta when I got him on the phone. I explained the situation and he said he needed to make a phone call and he would call me back. An hour or so later, the phone rang. It was my friend, the tour operator. He informed me our group would be able to see the Sistine Chapel the next morning. He gave us a door number and told us to be there promptly at 8:00 a.m. the next morning. We were at the door at 8:00 and the door was opened for us. We got a first class tour of the Chapel, a trip to the airport on time, and everybody was happy!

The tour members on one of my trips had a very unusual experience. I woke up one morning and thought it was still night. The reason? A sand storm had hit during the night. The sky was dark. I had never seen a sand storm. Then another strange quirk of weather came our way.

When we were packing getting ready to go to the airport to board our plane to Athens, Greece, we were told five inches of snow were expected in Jerusalem. This was most unusual. It is a rare thing for Jerusalem to get a snowfall, and especially rare to get five inches. Our bus driver had never driven in snow. He was driving a $150,000 bus which was not his. So he took it very slow all the way to Tel Aviv, a distance of about 45 miles. He drove at a speed of 10 to 15 MPH. We missed our flight. We did get to the airport in Tel Aviv in time to catch a charter flight which we took to Athens.

18

On being Mrs. Wildmon's husband

The Scriptures give us a clear picture of the disciple Andrew. He is always mentioned after his brother Peter. I believe the life of Andrew gives us information on how to be second best. Lots of people never learn to be a good number two. Years ago Avis car rental had an ad saying Avis had to try harder because they were number two. Andrew knew how to be number two.

After Lynda graduated from college, she got a job teaching home economics at the school in the little community of Plato, Missouri, about twenty miles from Fort Leonard Wood where I was stationed. I asked for, and was granted, permission to live off base when I was in the Army. We rented a small mobile home about fifty yards from Lynda's classroom. I used the car to go to the base and Lynda walked to her job. We had a scare one day while Lynda was preparing lunch. Something happened when she plugged in a small appliance. The outlet shot an electric flash across the room. The shock knocked Lynda to the floor. She was unharmed, but we worried because she was pregnant with Tim.

The mobile home we rented (for $100 a month, which was a high price) was eight feet wide and 32 feet long. Quick figuring says that comes out at 256 square feet. Our current den is larger than that. I had an old television set with a 10-inch screen which I purchased for $10 while I was in college. In my free time I built a cabinet for the set and we enjoyed receiving the one station in Springfield, Missouri. Lynda's income helped us financially. With her income and my small salary from the Army, we did relatively well.

One of the things I had to get accustomed to was the way I was addressed by the students and people in the community. Up to this point in our marriage, here is the way the introduction went: "Here's Don, and this is Lynda, Don's wife." That soon changed, and I got used to the change. Here is the way I was introduced by the students and the people in the community: "Here's Mrs. Wildmon, the home economics teacher, and here is Mrs. Wildmon's husband."

The weather was something else we had to learn to live with. This was in the winter of 1962. On one occasion it came a big snow and ice storm. The temperature fell below the zero degrees. I recall asking the clerk at the town store what the weather would do that day. He said it was supposed to warm up, getting as high as four degrees above zero.

While in the Army, we became good friends with a couple from Texas. He was a basketball coach and she was a teacher. So you can see we had much in common. After we were out of the Army and back in Mississippi preaching at three small churches, we visited with the couple. We drove to El Paso, Texas, and had a good time rehashing the time we shared at Fort Leonard Wood. Having no money to rent a motel room, we bought a tent and spent most nights sleeping in the tent. We carried Tim and Angela with us, along with Lynda's younger sister and brother. That experience caused us to almost give up camping.

Like Andrew I learned to be second best. Being second best did not change my relationship with Lynda.

19

Arguing with a computer is fruitless

In my many travels around the nation, I spent a lot of time reading the on-board magazines from each airline. There was always one ad that appeared in nearly every on-board magazine. The ad was promoting something I had never heard of. It was an ad for something called a "word processor." A couple of years passed before I asked a friend of mine what a word processor was. He explained it was a computer-like machine that helped make work better and faster than a typewriter.

Seeing how much AFA would be using a word processor, I ordered one at a cost of $16,000. Years later I was able to buy 10 of the word processors for $400 each. They were old, but they ran well and hardly ever gave us any problem.

I was told it would be about a month before the word processor would be delivered. I asked for some information on the word processor. I was sent a book about how the word processer worked. I carried it home and decided to study the book so I would know how to operate it. I studied that operating manual each night.

About a week from when the new machine was to be delivered, I felt I had the operating instructions down pat. This was no easy task. Why? Because the operating manual had many words that were foreign to me. They were technical words.

The day the word processor was delivered, we set it up and the IBM representatives walked us through various programs. After the representatives were gone, I sat down to see if I understood everything they had shown us. I worked on the word processor until it was time to go home. That night I got my instruction book out and read it through one more time. The next morning I sat down and began running the various programs. Everything worked just fine until I hit a snag near the end of the instruction book.

I worked on the problem again and again. I got some of the office personnel to read the instructions and try to get the program to run. Still no luck. After becoming totally frustrated, when it came quitting time, I was exhausted. I took the instruction manual home with me. I studied the book again.

The next morning, I tried at the office again. I tried two more times. Still no luck. So I called IBM and told them my problem. I asked the IBM reps to try to run the program. They said they would look into the problem and get back with me. By the time all of this expired, I had been working on this same problem nearly three frustrating days.

Have you ever had a similar experience? You do what the instructions tell you to do. But the computer still refuses to obey your command. That makes you angry. Then you get tired of trying to get the computer to reply and it keeps sending back the wrong answer. One thing I have learned about computers is they will not argue with you. It is either the computer's way or the highway.

Later that day IBM called to tell me they had found the problem. What was the problem that ruined three days for me? Hold your breath.

The instructions in the instruction book were wrong!

20

I nearly got caught hitch-hiking home

When I was in the Army I would try to get home as often as I could. Since we shared one car, sometimes Lynda would take it to school and sometimes I would take it to Fort Leonard Wood, Missouri. At other times I could often catch a ride with buddies who lived near me in northeast Mississippi. It was about a seven hour drive from the army base to Tupelo.

Each Friday ten soldiers would report to the company headquarters for inspection. These soldiers were selected to pull guard duty for the coming weekend. The soldiers would line up for inspection. Out of the ten soldiers, the one who dressed most impressive and answered standard questions best would get the weekend off. The soldier who was the sharpest was known as the "Super." Several times while I was in the army, I was chosen Super. I had one pair of boots I wore only when selected for guard duty. They really shined. I used Johnson liquid floor wax to keep them shining. All my friends would ask to borrow my boots when they tried out for Super.

On one occasion I won "Super" and got the weekend off. Even as "Super" I still was not allowed to leave the base. Despite that, I decided to go home for the weekend. The only problem was I didn't have the car nor enough money to buy a bus ticket to Columbus, Mississippi. I decided I would hitch-hike to Columbus. I did this knowing I was running a risk. If I was caught off base, I was in trouble. Nevertheless, I decided to try it. I got a buddy to cover for me at roll call, and to take me approximately fifteen miles to the back gate of the army base.

I caught a ride on the little used country road leading to the main highway. On the main highway I stood on the side of the road and waited for a car. It was about noon. I waited. Finally, a car was in sight. But it passed me by. After a while, there was another car. It too passed me by. In fact, no one stopped to pick me up. I stood on the highway for a couple of hours. I knew it would not be long until it would begin to get dark. And when it was dark, there was no hope of catching a ride. I had enough money to catch a bus to Memphis from Rolla, Missouri, which was a few miles north from where I was. I did catch a ride to Rolla and purchased the ticket to Memphis. The problem was after I purchased the ticket, I only had 10-cents left. I caught the next bus to St. Louis, where I was to transfer to the bus to Memphis.

The bus from Rolla arrived in St. Louis about 8:00 p.m. My bus to Memphis was scheduled to leave at 11:00 p.m. I spent time reading a newspaper left on a bench while waiting for the bus. As I looked across the bus station, I noticed two Military Police making their rounds and seeing if there were any military personnel who should not be there. This presented a major problem for me. I was wearing my military khaki pants and military shoes. They were a dead give away. The MP's headed toward me. I sat on the bench holding the newspaper in front of me, pretending I was reading it. I sat still and didn't move. They came within about ten feet of me. Lucky for me, they never came my way.

The bus to Memphis was scheduled to leave at 11:00 p.m. I was keeping a pretty good eye on my watch. At about 10:45, I asked the lady at the ticket window when the bus to Memphis was leaving. She told me it left nearly an hour earlier. The problem was my watch was set on standard time and St. Louis was on daylight saving time. I caught the next bus out and got to Memphis in mid-morning. The bus station was downtown and I needed to get out to the highway on the outskirts of town. In my pocket I had one dime. I got on the city bus (the fare was 10-cents) and rode to the end of the line, where the city ended and the highway began.

I managed to hitch-hike from Memphis to Columbus, Mississippi, getting there late in the afternoon. I decided my hitch-hiking days were over. Besides, due to the cultural change, it would soon become too dangerous to hitch-hike.

21

Overriding the bishop and his staff

As a United Methodist minister, my career was totally in my bishop's hands, as were all United Methodist pastors. The bishop makes all the appointments, with the help of his district superintendents. The bishop decides what minister serves which church. Translated, that meant the bishop indirectly controlled what a ministers salary would be, where a minister's children would attend school, the house the pastor's family would live in, the kind of car he or she would drive, etc.

The house in which the minister lives belongs to the conference. The minister often has built up no equity toward the purchase of a home during his years of ministry. And since their salaries are usually below other professions, it is difficult to save enough to purchase a home. In other words, it is best to stay on the bishop's good side.

Often when the conference (geographical area) needed extra income they would have a "capital funds campaign." The capital funds campaign was an effort to raise additional funds outside the normal channels.

In my conference, the bishop and his superintendents prepared a capital funds campaign to raise money for a college and a few other causes. Despite a great need to help retired ministers, their cause was not included in the capital funds campaign. When questioned about leaving retired ministers out of the effort, the conference leaders said the next campaign would be a capital funds campaign for retired ministers only.

In 1976 the bishop and his cabinet (superintendents) decided the conference needed the capital funds campaign to raise money for the retired ministers. However, there was a catch. The retired minister's fund would not be the only recipient. This despite the earlier promise made concerning the retired ministers. Retired ministries often didn't have enough income despite years of giving their best.

Upon hearing what the leaders of my conference planned to do, I decided I would face the conference leaders and oppose their plan. And I would have some experience to help me.

About a year before the leaders made the decision to propose the campaign to aid the retired ministers, the leaders had proposed a plan to reorganize the districts in the conference. I did not think the plan would do what it proposed to do. I went to a close friend who happened to be my superintendent. I told my superintendent of my plans to oppose the reorganization. When the meeting to reorganize the districts came, I spoke against the proposal.

But the leaders were prepared. Prior to the meeting, my superintendent had told the bishop and other leaders of my plan. When the vote on the reorganization came, I lost. The vote wasn't even close. I looked like a fool. But the loss helped win a victory in my struggle to honor a promise made to retired ministers. I learned to be prepared, to do my homework, and not to broadcast my plans.

About a year later, the conference met to vote on the promise made to the retired ministers. At the conference when the motion to vote on the capital funds campaign came to the floor, I was one of the first to speak. I reminded the conference members of the promise made concerning the retired ministers. I made a strong plea for the conference to honor the promise. I got a round of applause when I sat down.

The leaders of the conference had their plan to oppose me. One by one the leaders made their way to the microphone to make their plea. After each one, I would go to the microphone and refute what was said. The bishop would rule me out of order and I would sit down. Then another leader would speak and I would respond. The bishop would rule me out of order and I would sit down.

Then the bishop did something extraordinary! He got out of the chair and asked one of his superintendents to take his place. Under Roberts Rules of Order, the bishop had to leave the chair before he could speak to the conference. The bishop made a lengthy, passionate plea for support. He then returned to the chair and called for the vote. The vote was overwhelming! My work had won a victory for the retired ministers. What was the bishop's response toward me? The bishop asked me to head up the top conference program for the coming year.

22

Chuck Colson congratulates Don

One of the most cherished letters I ever received came from Chuck Colson. Chuck is gone now, but his influence will go on through the ages. I cherish the letter because of who wrote it. That Don Wildmon should get a letter from Chuck Colson thanking him for founding AFA is just unreal. That someone who stood head and shoulders over all the characters of Watergate should write me, and especially say some kind words about me, is nearly shouting material.

I don't consider myself worthy to even be in the same ball park with this very humble servant of God. I never met Chuck in person. Our paths just never did pass. I wish they had, but I have his letter hanging in the entrance at our AFA Headquarters to remind me of his work for the Lord.

His letter to me is as follows.

March 11, 2010
Dear Don,

I just read in the New York Times that you are stepping down as Chairman of the American Family Association. That saddens me greatly, but I was happy to note that your son Tim will be leading the ministry.

You have done a phenomenal job, Don. You've produced a very, very powerful movement; that's a term I use advisedly because I think it's much more important to fuel movements than to start organizations.

I had a pretty good taste of how influential you've become when I compared the results in signatures to the Manhattan Declaration from your list and the list of other organizations. What a legacy you have created for your own ministry, and life.

I remember being in Canada a few years ago, and the Chaplain General of the prisons said that I was a remarkably blessed man because I was living long enough to see the fruits of my ministry. That could certainly be said about you, Don. The thing for which you should have particular gratitude is that you've seen the impact in what is maybe the most crucial area of public policy today. It's hard to imagine anything more important than the preservation of life and the preservation of the family. You have been right on the front lines, and have made and are making a terrific impact on our country.

I know God brought you through a horrible experience and has kept you alive for His purpose. So seek it every day; live it out with gratitude; and continue to give us the benefit of your wisdom and leadership.

God bless you, Don.

Yours in His service,
Charles W. Colson

23

Don: jack of all trades, master of none

I was born in the little community of Dumas, Mississippi, the son of a Christian farmer father and a Christian mother. I was born on a very cold January day before the doctor could arrive. I was delivered by a nurse who was a friend of the family. Years later, I would conduct her funeral.

I was the baby, having two brothers, Johnny and Allen, and two sisters, Helen and Louise. When I was age two, our family moved to the small town of Ripley, Mississippi. I was destined to live the next 16 years growing up in Ripley. While growing up I found many places to work and earn some money so I could enjoy the activities others enjoyed.

While not poor, the Wildmon family was very limited in financial resources. Our parents lost their 100 acre farm when they had three bad crop years in a row. But there was love in the family, and the family could be found at the church building when the doors opened.

I worked at a service station washing cars, in a shoe store selling shoes, and in a theatre running the projector. While in high school I delivered two morning newspapers (circulation about 300 papers) every morning beginning about 4:00 a.m.

I started driving at age thirteen. The local police chief had two boys who were my friends, so the chief looked the other way when I was driving.

I was a fairly good football player, even though I weighed only 130 pounds soaking wet. I played half-back on an undefeated team. I was the third son of the family who had played that position and wore the same jersey number.

I was a reasonably intelligent person, but didn't take my studies too seriously. I could, at times, take a stand for something I truly believed. In my senior year I was dismissed from my English class when I thought another student was being favored. I refused to apologize to the teacher, believing I was in the right, but it cost me my diploma. She was a very good teacher and I really liked her.

In order to graduate with my classmates, I was required to take a correspondence course. At the time for the graduation exercise, I had not heard from my correspondence course. I wasn't allowed to graduate with my class. I was, however, allowed to participate in the graduation exercises, even walking across the stage to receive a diploma book without a diploma. The audience didn't know I did not get a diploma.

From age nine, I always felt God had something "special" He wanted me to do. But I did not speak of it often. First, because it could be interpreted by some as me having a connection to God others did not have. And, second, I did not think of myself as being a better Christian than those who share a common calling.

When I enrolled at Mississippi State University in the fall of 1956, "Mama Wildmon," as she was affectionately called, went with me to register. She visited one of the Deans and asked about my vocational abilities. The Dean told Mama Wildmon I could do just about anything I wanted to do. Of course, that isn't really what the Dean told Mama Wildmon. What he had told her, in reality, was I could fit well in several occupations. But the "mama" was inside Mama Wildmon and she heard the dean say what she wanted to hear him say. After all, I was Mama Wildmon's baby boy.

24

God increases our 30 picketers to 1,000

How do you convince a multi-billion dollar TV network to change their programming? After talking with the networks for nearly a year, I finally found a way to get their attention. It was through their pocketbook. Plead with them all you want, unless they feel it in their pocketbook, all your efforts will be fruitless.

I searched for a method of identifying the leading sponsors of sex, violence and profanity. I decided I would monitor the network shows for three months during prime-time and ask for a boycott of the leading sponsors of sex, violence and profanity. If advertisers cut off the funding for the offensive programs, the programs would no longer be on the air.

So from our small but growing numbers of supporters, we put together twenty monitoring teams of twenty-one people each, from nineteen states. We had 20 individuals monitoring each night during prime-time, seven nights a week. With the monitoring we could gather a lot of information: how much sex, violence and profanity was aired, what companies sponsored the most sex, violence and profanity, what programs contained the most sex, violence and profanity.

After monitoring was complete, we had a really big surprise. One company at the top of the list was none other than Sears. Now, at that time in our nation's history Sears was one company which supported family values. We could not have picked a better company to boycott. We released the findings of the monitoring and released the results. In addition to Sears, other family-friendly companies ended up on the top ten list.

Within a matter of days the monitoring was making big waves in the media. We decided to call for a boycott of Sears. We had some correspondence with Sears, both on the phone and in letters. We scheduled a nationwide picketing of Sears for May 13. After we announced the boycott and the picketing, Sears called and wanted to visit with us in Tupelo.

Once the day for the meeting had been set, we faced a problem: where do we meet? You see, AFA had no office space. I was working from my home, having turned my dining room into an office. We didn't want these visitors to think we were a one man show. Money was short so I didn't want to spend $80 for a business room at the hotel. Finally, a friend who was serving my previous church offered his study in which to meet.

Two representatives arrived at the airport and my brother Allen met them and brought them to the church. We had a good discussion, but felt little was accomplished. They were aware of the upcoming boycott, and also aware of our scheduled picketing. They gave little impression they were going to change their TV advertising policy. We shook hands and parted ways. Allen took them to the airport.

We set the date for the picketing. I flew to Chicago the day before our small group could make plans concerning the upcoming picket that night. The next day we left early to make sure we got to the Sears Tower in plenty of time. We met the others who were coming from another part of the city. All together, there were about 30 who had come to participate. Each of us had a picket sign reading "Boycott Sears." We had trained our people to be nice to the Sears personnel at the various stores. Sears had instructed their people to do the same. At some of the Sears stores they brought lemonade and cookies to the picketers.

In front of the Sears building in Chicago was a wide open plaza which would hold about one thousand people. When I set the time for the picket, I set it for noon in all the approximately 100 cities where

Sears had a store. At about five minutes before noon each of us began walking back and forth in front of the Sears Tower. But all of a sudden something happened which we never could have planned.

Hundreds of Sears employees began piling out of the Tower to the big plaza. There we were, all thirty of us, spread out over the entire plaza. I did not know those employees would all come out of the front doors at noon. Neither did I know television crews from all the networks were already gathering their shots for national exposure. When the film was used that night, it showed hundreds of Sears employees mixed with our thirty picketers. The viewer, seeing the crowd, assumed those hundreds of Sears employee were picketers.

While we were picketing, I was approached by a network reporter and asked if I had heard the news. I asked him what news. He said Sears had issued a press released saying they were withdrawing their advertising from **Three's Company** and **Charlie's Angels**, two programs known for their sex and violence. Driving from the Memphis Airport home that night, I listened to the news. It was the lead story.

You know, I think maybe God was using His sense of humor. God took thirty picketers and multiplied them a hundred fold, just like what Jesus said.

25

Don honored by two institutions
of higher learning

I have been honored by two greatly respected institutions of higher education. On May 24, 1990 Asbury College in Wilmore, Kentucky, honored me with a Doctor of Laws degree. On October 2, 1994 Wesley Biblical Seminary in Jackson, Mississippi, honored me with a Doctor of Divinity degree.

Below are the inscriptions which were read at the ceremonies honoring me. I was deeply moved by these honors. I also appreciate the great work both schools are doing in preparing their students to serve God and serve man.

※⊱⊰※

Remarks made by Dr. Dennis Kinlaw, President of Asbury College:

In the course of human history, God has shown His grace to His children in many ways. One of those ways is in His gift of prophets. Anyone who knows the history of Israel will understand. Sometimes the prophets stood in prominent places and were part of the royal court, like Isaiah. At other times, they came from the wilderness like John the Baptist and Amos. Some knew some measure of success.

Others were slaughtered for their fidelity to the Word which had been given them. Regardless of their fate, the world was the better for their courage and outspokenness. Today God has looked with favor upon us and has given to our country again a prophet.

This one came not from the courts, not from the wilderness but from Tupelo, Mississippi. A United Methodist preacher, his national role began with a project in his own congregation called "Turn-Off-The-TV-Week." Offended by the deadly effect of network television on moral and ethical sensitivities and its general hostility to all of the human mysteries Christians call sacred, Donald Wildmon asked his people to shut off their TV sets for a week and call their local stations and explain why.

That action in Southaven, Mississippi, by a single congregation and its pastor received instant media attention. Donald Wildmon has struck a very sensitive nerve. The result during these last 13 years, have been surprising. We have seen again the power of one single voice, evolved by God, to touch the conscience of a nation. From his office in Tupelo, Mississippi, through his witness and that of his American Family Association, he has caused the major networks to remove some programs and drastically edit others. You may not be pleased with what you find on your TV screens today. Let me simply say the diet would be infinitely worse were it not for him.

In 1986 his activities caused one major magazine, a pioneer in the popularization of the erotic, to drop its sales some 674,000 copies a month. Last year *Advertising Age* and *Election Media* indicated that Wildmon's Christian Leaders for Responsible Television had caused the networks to lose millions in revenues from advertisers. Feeling the heat, the advertisers have backed away from shows that they consider "potentially offensive."

Needless to say, Don Wildmon's outspokenness has not made him popular. His honesty and his convictions have brought him scorn, contumely, and open hostility. Today he is the defendant in a million dollar lawsuit provoked by his concern for righteousness.

The God of Scriptures is the God who does the unlikely. No

one expected a ruddy-faced lad with a sling from the village of Bethlehem to be the means of delivering from the bondage imposed by the Philistines with their heavily armed Goliath. Nor did many of us expect a prophet of God out of Tupelo, Mississippi. But God has given us one. And today we at Asbury College give thanks.

So, in view of your distinctive leadership and contributions to the cause of righteousness, by the authority vested in me by the Board of Trustees of Asbury College, I confer upon you, Donald E. Wildmon, the honorary degree of Doctor of Laws, with all the rights and privileges pertaining thereto.

Remarks made by Dr. Harold Spann, President of Wesley Biblical Seminary:

In this age of catastrophic moral deterioration and erosion of basic values, one voice has spoken out with greater clarity and faithfulness than perhaps any other. The voice is that of Dr. Donald E. Wildmon, founder/president of the American Family Association.

The American Family Association is a Christian organization promoting the Christian ethic in society with special emphasis on the media. Founded in June 1977, the AFA is a citizen's group not affiliated with any other organization or religious denomination. While Dr. Wildmon maintains his ministerial relations with the United Methodist Church and serves under special appointment by his denomination, AFA is in no way affiliated with the United Methodist Church nor any other denomination. Educated at Millsaps College and Emory University, he also received in 1990 the Doctor of Laws degree honorary from Asbury College.

Before founding the AFA, he served United Methodist pastorates in Mississippi. These include Iuka Circuit, Lee Acres in Tupelo and First United Methodist Church in Southaven.

From 1961-1963, Dr. Wildmon served with the United States

Army, Special Services section at Fort Leonard Wood, Missouri.

He is author of 22 books with more than 500,000 copies in print.

His heroic and well-informed stand against pornography and other evils that threaten the American home and family has brought him to national attention, thus widening and multiplying the effectiveness of Dr. Wildmon and his full-time staff of 50, including the AFA Legal Center with a staff of five attorneys. The monthly AFA Journal has a circulation of approximately 750,000.

Dr. Wildmon has appeared on **Meet the Press, MacNeil Lehrer Report, Good Morning America, The Tomorrow Show, The Today Show, Nightline, Inside Story, 700 Club, Donahue,** and several other syndicated and local programs and has been featured in *Family Weekly, TV Guide, Time, Newsweek, People* (twice), *Saturday Evening Post, Our Sunday Visitor, Christianity Today, Christian Herald, Wall Street Journal* and other publications.

The AFA crusade for Christian values and those values in particular that are essential for the American home and family, has been more instrumental in bringing preservation of major businesses promoting pornography to recognize that their best interests are not served by contributing to the moral demise of our nation. Some have been influenced to abandon their pornographic sales.

Often honored, frequently applauded, but in many cases opposed and assailed, the man we honor tonight merits the gratitude and honor of all Christian people in this land. Wesley Biblical Seminary gladly asserts its stand alongside Donald Wildmon, his family and his organization because the Seminary is committed to the same causes represented by the AFA. In fact, this conservative, Biblical, Wesleyan-Arminian institution honors itself in a most significant way by honoring Dr. Wildmon.

It gives the Board of Trustees, the administration, faculty, staff and students great delight to recognize and honor him as we do this evening.

It has been wisely expressed that an institution is the lengthening shadow of a man. In this case, the shadow cast upon our society on one of the noblest crusades of our time is one whose length, breadth and quality defy appropriate definition. When the history of this era is recorded, especially its Christian history, the name of our honoree will stand forth in bold relief and noble dignity and honor.

By the authority vested in me by the Board of Trustees of Wesley Biblical Seminary and by the State of Mississippi, I confer upon you, Donald E. Wildmon, the degree of Doctor of Divinity with all the rights and privileges pertaining thereunto.

26

A case of mistaken identity

BY ALLEN WILDMON

I was on my knees in the dirt in the schoolyard shooting marbles with a couple of buddies. We were in grade school, and Don was a few years behind me. We were young and our mother was teaching first grade in the small county school of Walnut, Mississippi.

I was just getting ready to push my thumb forward with fervor in order to disperse as many marbles as possible from the ring when someone tapped me on the shoulder and said, "Come with me."

I looked up from my bent-knee stance at the tall figure looking down at me. It was the principal of the school, Mr. Jackson. I replied:

"Yes Sir, but what for?"

"Mrs. Wildmon said you started a fight with another boy, so come with me."

"Mr. Jackson, I didn't do anything, and I haven't started a fight."

"Do as I say, and come with me!" He said in a somewhat stern tone of voice.

When we reached his office, he opened the big brown desk drawer and retrieved a small paddle made of light colored wood.

"Lean over my desk," he said.

"But sir, I promise that I didn't start a fight," I said as I started to cry.

"Do as I say." He responded.

"Yes sir, I replied as I leaned over his desk, and he proceeded to give me three light licks with the paddle.

"You may go now, and don't pick any more fights." I turned my back and left as quickly as possible. I headed straight to my mother's first grade classroom.

I opened her classroom door and entered; since it was recess, she was all alone sitting at her desk looking at a poster of a horse one of her pupils had drawn. "Mama, Mr. Jackson just gave me a paddling."

"Paddling! What for?"

"He said you told him I started a fight."

"I'm so sorry," she said as she reached down and hugged me. "Don was the one who started the fight. You two look so much alike, I guess he got the two of you mixed up." This helped my feelings, and I left her room to find my buddies to finish our marble game.

As we grew older many people got Don's and my identities confused. Even Don's grandson would come by the AFA office, reach for me and call me Pa Pa.

27

One mean Mississippi mosquito

I will always remember August 15, 2009. While trying to get a pool umbrella in place, I finally gave up and went into the house to cool off. It was nearly 100 degrees outside and I was exhausted from trying to put the 10-foot crooked umbrella pole into place. It would be a day I will remember the rest of my life.

I sat down on the couch next to Lynda and remarked it was extremely hot outside. I knew I was tired but I thought that it was simply from trying to get the pole in place. Then I dozed off to sleep.

Everything seemed okay for the rest of that day. Sunday I got dressed for church and sat down, waiting on Lynda to get ready. When she said she was ready, I remarked I didn't feel well. I told Lynda I didn't feel like going. I lay around the house for the rest of the day.

On Monday, I was out of town with my son for the day. We did not get home until late in the afternoon. I was in my recliner when I began shaking. Finally the rigors ended. I felt rather weak, so I ate and then went to bed.

On Tuesday, I went to work but came home after about an hour and went to bed. Tuesday evening we went to the emergency room. We left after three hours without seeing a doctor or without a diagnosis of my illness.

On Wednesday I went to see the doctor who thought, for good reason, I had a kidney infection. I had no pain. I was simply weak and did not feel like doing anything other than sleeping.

On Thursday I spent most of the day sleeping.

On Friday, after I told Tim and Donna I was seeing double, they carried me to the emergency room again. This time there was a doctor. After examining me, the doctor said he could not find anything to worry about. He was preparing to release me and let me go home.

It so happened a very close family friend, who was also a nurse, was in the room at the same time as the doctor. The friend was surprised that the doctor was going to release me. "You are going to admit him, aren't you?" our friend asked. "Well, I will see what's available. I will try to get him a room," the doctor replied.

We were taken to a room. When things settled down, the children went home and Lynda stayed. During the night I began shaking again. This time it was bad. It was all Lynda could do to keep me on the bed. She thought I could be having a seizure. Two times during the night, as the shaking did not stop, Lynda went to the nurse's station and requested help. She was told there was nothing they could do until the doctor got there in the morning.

About 2:00 in the morning, with the room dark and while Lynda was struggling to keep me on the bed, the door opened and a familiar body walked toward Lynda. It was Donna, "I couldn't sleep worrying about Daddy," she said. "I couldn't sleep so I decided to come down and check on him." Donna lives about 20 miles from the hospital. Lynda said Donna was the closest thing to an angel she had ever seen.

Lynda told Donna about the situation, that she was not getting much attention from the nurses. About that time, a nurse came into the room. Donna told the nurse to get an ambulance ready, she was taking her father to Memphis.

In a short time it was apparent the nurse needed to get someone higher up to handle the situation, and she needed to do it fast. Earlier, Lynda had been told there was not a doctor available. The nurse left rather quickly. In a short time, lo and behold, there was a doctor in the room. The doctor checked me out and then ordered me taken to intensive care. She told Lynda she was going to give me several antibiotics because she didn't know what was wrong with me.

The next morning the doctors (there were several by mid-morning) ran several tests, starting with a spinal tap. They first though I had viral meningitis. For about a week the doctors kept running tests and searching for some cause. Blood work and other information was sent to Mayo Clinic in Rockford, Minnesota. In a few days we got word from the Mayo Clinic. Three of five tests at Mayo said it was St. Louis encephalitis and two said it was West Nile encephalitis. They again sent information to Mayo. In two days Mayo replied. Mayo this time said the results were similar. I stayed in intensive care for about fifteen days. Since there was nothing they could do for encephalitis, they were making sure nothing worse happened. We had a great team of doctors that worked together to give us excellent cared.

After about a week or so, the doctor chatted with Lynda about my medical situation. The doctor gave Lynda her (the doctor) honest opinion , : the doctor said, "It's in God's hands now." I did improve enough to be moved to a step-down floor, a unit that provided special care. I stayed in North Mississippi Medical Center until September 20, before going to Methodist Hospital in Jackson, Mississippi, to go through a month of rehab. When I started my rehab, I was confined to a wheelchair. In addition to the physical aspect of rehab, I was also being treated with some experimental drugs. I had many awful dreams because of the drugs.

When it became apparent I was being given experimental drugs, Donna sent a note to one of the doctors that they were not to give me any more. Perhaps my body had absorbed so much of these drugs that it would take months to get them out of my system. The drugs left me totally confused. Lynda said I was incoherent. I did not respond to the treatment. The doctor saw they were having an adverse effect.

In one of the dreams I was fleeing from a man who was trying to kill me and cut my body into pieces. Here is something of a mystery to me. In my dreams I could talk with people outside the dream, but not with anyone inside the dream. In other words I could talk with Lynda, but not talk with anyone in my dream. In the dream where the man was trying to cut me into pieces, I begged and pleaded with Lynda to call 911, but she kept telling me there was no one in the room with us. I knew there was someone because he was trying to kill us, put us in body bags and check them through security at the airport.

In another dream, I thought I had ruined a man's wheelchair, and I was trying to get Lynda to give me enough money to buy him a new one. In another dream near Christmas, I saw three children with their faces flush against the window. I asked Lynda about them and she could not see them. I saw them, waved at them and asked Lynda to wave at them. In a few minutes the three small children had disappeared, but then they turned again sitting on a chair.

For months after being released from the hospital, speed limit signs all looked like a person's face, except it was square. In another dream, I had my 15-year-old grandson driving a truck loaded down with Christmas buttons. One dream, about a baseball team coming to Mississippi to play in a tourney, was so real that later I asked an employee if it was, indeed, real.

I spent a month in rehab at Methodist Hospital in Jackson, and then went to the rehab unit at the North Mississippi Medical Center. I spent a month in rehab at NMMC. I received exceptional care in both places.

All told I was in the hospital 123 days. Lynda was with me all the time, except when one of the children would cover for her for a night or so.

The first day after my discharge from the hospital, Lynda and I went to Memphis for a doctor's appointment with our ophthalmologist to check on my left eye. We invited my brother and sister and their spouses to meet us at a restaurant and share a meal. It was also the first day I had used my walker outside the hospital or home. I went to the restroom. Lynda also had to use the facility so I was waiting for her as she came out. In trying to answer my cell phone, I shifted my walker.

I misjudged when I turned the walker and fell backward. My head hit the wall with a solid, hard lick. I thought nothing about it. Just a hard lick. I got up and continued as things seemed normal.

When I first entered the hospital because of the mosquito bite, an MRI showed a small blood clot on my brain. The doctors said the blood clot wasn't a real big threat at that moment and we would just keep an eye on it.

A few weeks later I had to get another MRI for my ophthalmologist in Memphis. When the results came back, the blood clot had grown to a dangerous size. Surgery was scheduled for early the next morning. I never thought I would have my skull opened and my brain operated on, but everything went fine. We were glad when it was over.

That one little mosquito sure did cause me a whole lot of trouble. I spent four months in the hospital because of the mosquito. With the walking cane and walking slowly, I can get by. So I'm not complaining. I just thank God for pulling me through.

Yet I still faced the battle with the cancer in the back of my left eye.

While in the hospital recuperating, my yearly eye checkup came due. I was given the ok to leave the hospital to get the checkup. When the doctor finished with his tests, he gave Lynda and me his report. He said he saw something he had not seen before. He told us he would make an appointment with a specialist in Memphis to check it out more fully. He said he did not have the equipment necessary to do what was needed.

The day came for us to go to Memphis for the tests. I did not give it much thought. I certainly didn't worry about the outcome. Everything was going to be ok, and if it wasn't then the doctors had medicine and equipment to make it ok. When all the tests had been run, the doctor gave us the news: I had cancer (melanoma) behind my left eye and needed surgery.

I asked how the surgery would affect my sight. The doctor said if we did the surgery it would weaken the veins in my left eye which would eventually cause blindness in that eye. But if I did not have surgery, the cancer would spread. I had no choice.

The doctor explained that he would implant radioactive disks behind my left eye. They would stay there for eight days and then be removed.

So two days after Christmas Lynda and I went to Methodist Hospital in Memphis for surgery. Our stay would last eight days. During that time we would be confined to the hospital.

I remember lying on the stretcher in the holding room waiting to go into surgery. The doctor doing the surgery was not the one who had been treating me. She asked me a few questions to break the ice. She then picked up my chart and began reading. She came down to my name, and paused. She looked at the chart, and then looked at me. "Are you *the* Don Wildmon," she asked. "Yes, doctor," I replied. "I get your magazine," she said. We chatted a little bit before the anesthesia took effect. The surgery went fine, no surprises.

Since the surgery, I have lost sight in my left eye. I still have about 70 percent use of my right eye, so it isn't as bad as it could have been. I can still drive (except at night) and manage to do ok except in heavy traffic.

One thing I have learned in this ordeal. Thank God for your eyesight.

28

Mormons invite me to become a Mormon

I saw them coming down the driveway. They were neatly dressed, white shirts and dark pants. Their Bibles in their hands. They usually knock on our door at least once a year. I expect they have knocked on nearly every door in North America. I believe that is one of the reasons they have one of the fastest growing churches in the nation.

The two young boys were members of the Church of Latter-Day Saints, better known as Mormons. They were visiting all the houses in our area. And our house was one of them. It was extremely hot outside. So when they knocked on the door, we invited them in. They introduced themselves and their mission. Lynda asked if they would like some ice cold lemonade and some homemade cookies. They didn't refuse. In fact, you could tell they really liked the refreshments.

They began telling us what their mission was, and I told them I was very familiar with the Mormons. I explained to the young boys, probably about 20 years old, that I was a United Methodist minister. We never got into a discussion of religion. But we talked about other things. In fact, the young visitors probably stayed and visited for about an hour and half.

They asked several questions about my limping. I explained that it was caused by the St. Louis encephalitis I got when a mosquito bit me. I told them I had spent four months in the hospital and was still recovering from the mosquito bite. During the discussions Lynda refilled their lemonade glasses. Lynda and I asked the missionaries several questions about the work they do, how long they serve, how much money it takes, how often do they change locations, and several other such questions. As they were leaving, they wanted to know if they could visit with us again in the future. We told them they were welcome anytime they desired to visit. They visited a few more times before they were sent to a new assignment. They even brought us some home baked cookies.

A few weeks later, my secretary answered a call wanting to know if that caller could visit with me. Answering in the affirmative, the caller said he would call back later and follow up. Several weeks went by before the caller called again. Again, the same request. But the caller did say he had something he wanted to give to me.

The two young Mormons came to visit us again in a few weeks. They were relaxed and felt they were welcome to spend some time visiting with the Wildmons. They enjoyed discussing current events, moral issues and the future. They were very interesting young men. They probably spent about two hours visiting. And they enjoyed some more cold lemonade and home-baked cookies.

I appreciate the stand the Mormons take on family issues. They support marriage between one man and one woman, they are pro-life, and they basically have a very clean-cut lifestyle. The program they have in sending out young adults to do missionary work is a pattern which could help other churches.

Things rocked along for a few weeks before the person who said he had something to give me called again. He set a time and place to meet. He wanted to meet Lynda and me at the Mormon Church about four blocks from the AFA office. We set a time of mid-afternoon.

Lynda and I arrived a little early and waited. Neither Lynda nor I could imagine what it was that this gentleman wanted to give me.

Finally, those who were meeting with us arrived. We went into one of the classrooms. Each of the members of the other party introduced themselves. There were three men present, along with their wives. I introduced Lynda. Each of the gentlemen spoke giving the positions they held in their church. The men were leaders in the Mormon Church, serving as leaders in districts in Tennessee, Mississippi, and Alabama.

For about the next 30-40 minutes the discussion was centered toward me. There was a lull in the conversation before one of the leaders turned to me and said he would like to invite me to become a member of the Church of Jesus Christ of Latter-Day Saints. I was rather surprised at the invitation. Lynda, who was sitting behind me, said she would have liked to have seen my face when the invitation was given. I was presented a Mormon bible, the Book of Mormon, and other literature. This was something which caught me totally by surprise. I never expected something like this. I told the leaders I was humbled by the invitation, but would have to decline.

In one way, I did feel honored by the invitation. I obviously do not agree with the Mormon theology, but I am very much in favor of working with the Mormons, as well with other churches, in fighting a common foe.

29

You run into some strange situations when you travel

The pilot's voice came over the intercom. "Ladies and gentlemen, we are as happy to be here as you are."

When you travel a lot, you can have some interesting experiences to share. Such was the case with me on several occasions. Probably the one which stands out the most is a plane ride from Dallas to Memphis.

I had been in Denver for a meeting and was on my way home. When I arrived at the Denver airport I learned a tornado had passed near the DFW airport and all planes going into or out of DFW were grounded. Since DFW (Dallas-Fort Worth Airport) is one of the busiest airports in America, that action affected flights from scores of airports in the country. After about three hours of waiting, the plane from Denver to DFW was cleared to go. The flight from Denver to DFW was smooth, no problems.

Arriving at DFW, I saw mostly chaos. The terminals were filled with people trying to get out of DFW. Lines were long and, in some cases, tempers were short. I looked at the monitors to see if my flight to Memphis had been re-scheduled. It had not. Checking at one of the gates, I was told no time for departure had been set, but they would announce the departure time as soon as it was in place.

Finally, about four hours beyond the originally scheduled departure, the call came to board the flight to Memphis. That was good news to me. I got to the boarding gate, presented my boarding pass, and moved on to my seat. Everything went smooth with the liftoff. Finally, several hours late, I was on my way home. It was a good feeling.

After being in the air for about thirty minutes, the plane suddenly, and violently, hit turbulence. The impact caused the flight attendants to be thrown to the floor. People screamed. Looking out the window, I saw nothing but white. The lightning was that great. The plane was being jerked around like it was a toy. No word from the cockpit about what was going on and what we should expect. We were in the middle of the storm. And it was having no mercy.

We stayed in the storm for about thirty minutes. The shaking of the plane never ceased during that time, nor did the lightning. The lady in front of me prayed out loud, as did many others. Here I was, 30,000 feet above ground on a plane that felt like it would come apart at any minute. I was fully convinced I would never get off that plane alive. I thought about Lynda and the children. I had bought an insurance policy when the children were toddlers, so that should help them. I thought about never seeing them again on this earth. I thought about Lynda having to raise the children by herself.

Finally the plane was able to get out of the storm. We enjoyed smooth sailing all the way to Memphis. The lady in front of me told me that was the first time she had prayed in twenty years. Pulling up to the gate in Memphis, the pilot came over the speaker. "Ladies and gentlemen, we are as happy to be here as your are," he said. And that was all he said. His voice was trembling. The experience had shaken him, as it had all of the passengers.

Going to St. Louis, Getting to Detroit

On another occasion I was invited to speak to a group in St. Louis on a Saturday. I could get a flight from Memphis to St. Louis, give my speech and be back home that evening. Arriving at the airport late, I looked at the monitors to get the gate number, and rushed to the gate. I gave my boarding pass to the attendant and proceeded to my seat.

Waiting for the plane to depart, I began reading the on-board magazine.

I noticed for some reason the plane sat at the gate for a long time. Finally, the plane was pushed back and taxied to get in line for takeoff. I put the magazine in the pocket on the back of the seat in front of me and shut my eyes to take a short nap. I couldn't go to sleep, so I went back to reading. Since the flight from Memphis to St. Louis was only about an hour, I thought I would not be able to get much of a nap.

After being in the air for about an hour, I figured we were getting close to the time to be landing in St. Louis. I did notice it seemed we were in somewhat of a holding pattern for a long time. I waited to hear the announcement to get ready to land in St. Louis. But there was no announcement. Finally, the pilot told us we would be landing in about twenty minutes.

I looked at my watch. My speaking engagement was scheduled in about two hours. Once the plane landed, I would have to rush to get to the engagement on time. Breaking through the clouds, I looked out the window. What I saw was hard for me to believe. There was the airport. But there was a problem. It was not the St. Louis airport. I was landing in Detroit!

I had to get to a phone and let the people in St. Louis know I would not be making the speech. I did manage to get on the right plane to take me back to Memphis. And I did make it home.

A one day trip to Salt Lake City

I tried, in all my travels, to get the flights that would require the least amount of time away from home. On one occasion, I had a training seminar in Salt Lake City. I saw I could make flight arrangements to leave Memphis in the early morning, do the training and catch a late afternoon flight back to Memphis, then drive home and sleep in my own bed.

Getting up about four in the morning, I headed to Memphis, about 100 miles from my home in Tupelo. I got to the airport in plenty of time, boarded the plane, and got a nap on the non-stop flight to Salt Lake City. I was met at the airport in Salt Lake City by the leaders of the local group and they proceeded to go to the church where the training was being held. After finishing with the training, the host carried me back to the Salt Lake City airport. I caught my late afternoon flight back to Memphis, arriving at about nine that night.

Leaving the airport, I noticed my headlights were not as bright as they should be. No big deal, I said to myself, I can still see the road clearly. As I got on the highway leading home, I noticed the lights continued to get dimmer and dimmer. I managed to get to New Albany, about twenty-five miles from home. It was only a short time before the lights went completely out and the car stopped running. I managed to get the car off the the road. But it was about 2:00 in the morning. There was no moon. Everything was dark. Now what would I do? This was long before cell phones.

There was a mobile home about a half-mile away. I decided I would see if I could use their phone. I really didn't feel comfortable knocking on somebody's door at two in the morning. But I did. The response came from inside the mobile home: "Yeah, what do you want." I explained what had happened and asked if I could use his phone to call home. He let me in and I called home and explained to Lynda what had happened. I told her to let Tim come get me. I explained clearly where I was. Tim was about 16 years old at the time.

I thanked the man and went back to the car and waited. I knew it would be about forty-five minutes before Tim could get there. Very few cars or trucks passed at that time of night. About the time Tim should be getting to where I was, a truck appeared and close behind the truck was a car. The car was so close and going so fast, the person driving the car would have passed me without seeing my car.

Well, guess what happened. It was Tim and he did not see me. He kept going. There was nothing for me to do except wait. Since there was only one road from New Albany to Tupelo, Tim would be coming back by me. I waited about thirty minutes before Tim saw me on the side of the road as he was returning home.

When I got home, I went to bed. From that time forward, I did not try to make such a long trip in one day.

Locking the key in the car

Lynda and I once attended a planning retreat west of Denver. We flew into Denver, picked up a rental car and drove about two hours northwest. The meeting was being held at the summer home of a wealthy couple near Estes Park. It was built into the hillside of a mountain and had an absolutely beautiful view. We thoroughly enjoyed the time spent with others who shared our concern.

On the Sunday morning, when Lynda and I were scheduled to leave, we awoke to a six-inch snow as far as one could see. It was such a fantastic view. Since we don't have much snow down south, it was especially beautiful. And, with the snow, came cold weather. I decided to go out and start the engine and warm up the car. No problem. I inserted the key and started the engine. I got out and pushed the door closed. Just about the time I turned loose of the door, I remembered the key was in the ignition. I pulled the door handle. Locked. I went around and tried the door on the other side. Locked.

I went in and explained to the others what had happened. Well, I thought, I will just call the rental office at the airport in Denver. Then I remembered I always put the rental car papers above the sun visor. Now what do we do? Good question. I called the rental car's national reservation number found in the phone book. I called the number and was given another number. I was told to secure the serial number on the dashboard of the rental car. Then, after I had done that, I was given the number of a local locksmith. Remember now, this was on a Sunday morning. Locksmiths don't usually stay open on Sunday morning. I called but got no answer. Then, one of the other participants carried us into the small town. We found the locksmith's office and secured a home phone number. Making that call, we had to wait for him to get to his office. Since we didn't know how to tell the locksmith how to get to the house where we were staying, he had to follow us.

The locksmith made a key and it opened the door without any trouble. The engine was turned off. We thanked the gentleman and tried the key again before letting him go. After he left, I went out once again to start the engine. I put the key in, turned the starter, and started the engine. I pushed the door closed and then realized I had locked the key in the car again! But this time, I had put the extra key in my pocket And, yes, we did make our flight.

I know someone from Tupelo. He was a national speaker

In the fall of 2010 Lynda and her sister (Tam) and brother-in-law (Larry) and I visited Banff National Park in Canada. Banff is a beautiful place. And at the center of it all is Lake Louise. The Rockies are magnificent. I don't know which are the most beautiful, the Canadian Rockies or the Swiss Alps. We had a wonderful time at Banff.

We had one unusual incident to happen while there. We were all looking out at the beauty of Lake Louise. There was an elderly couple standing next to us. In a few minutes Tam, Larry and Lynda had struck up a conversation with the elderly couple. They talked for a few minutes and we learned the couple was from Montana. Larry told them we were from Tupelo, Mississippi.

"I knew someone from Tupelo, Mississippi. He was a national speaker," the elderly gentleman said. "Was it Elvis?" Larry asked.

"No, it wasn't Elvis. This person was a national speaker. I heard him years ago. It was a national meeting and he spoke. I remember that he was from Tupelo," he said.

Larry asked him if it was Don Wildmon. "Yes, that's who it was. Don Wildmon," he said. "Do you want to meet him?" Larry asked. "He is standing just behind you." We all thought it was something that seldom ever happens. Each of us, hundreds or even thousands, of miles from our separate homes, meeting like that. Travel does produce some strange situations.

I also know someone from Tupelo

On another flight, Lynda and I were flying from Memphis to Dallas-Fort Worth airport (DFW) when the young lady sitting next to me struck up a conversation. We began discussing where we were from and she told me the town where she lived. I told her I was from Tupelo. "The only person I know from Tupelo is Don Wildmon," she said. I waited a minute or so and then told her I was Don Wildmon. After we got off the plane in Dallas, she asked to have her picture taken with me.

I am glad I don't have a television ministry. I am uncomfortable when people call attention to me. Lynda and I are very humble people. After many years we still feel at home in small rural churches.

30

AFA drops 7-Eleven porn magazine sales 43% in one day

Early in my ministry I came to the conclusion, in my opinion, that soft-core pornography, such as *Playboy* and similar magazines, were as dangerous as hard-core porn. *Playboy* type magazines open the door to more hard core porn, just as marijuana opens the door to harder drugs. *Playboy* is more accepted by the 'intellectual.' We did some research to see which companies were big-time porn operators. It came as a surprise to learn which company was the largest distributor of porn in America. According to *Everybody's Business*, an almanac published by Harper and Row, the world's largest retailer of pornographic magazines was Dallas-based Southland Corporation. At the time the company owned and franchised more than 7,500 friendly, neighborhood 7-Eleven convenience stores.

7-Eleven says they are the good guys

This was particularly galling because I had seen print advertising and letters written by 7-Eleven officials calling their stores "family-oriented" establishments. And yet they were the biggest seller of magazines that attack virtually everything the family stands for. In January 1983 I decided 7-Eleven needed to be encouraged to live up to its claim. And I figured we were the ones to do it. So I asked AFA friends to hit 7-Eleven officials with a round of courteous communication, both by phone and letter. Our message? Please stop selling pornographic magazines!

Thousands of AFA supporters rallied to the cause. Consequently I wasn't surprised to hear from Allen Liles, Southland's vice president for public relations. When he asked if we could get together in Tupelo, I figured he had smelled smoke and wanted to snuff it out before our initial low-key protest effort spread into a full-scale fire.

Of course I knew that meant I'd get to hear Liles tell me what a wonderful company Southland is. Here's a condensed version of the usual public relations spiel: "Rev. Wildmon, you must be mistaken. You can't possibly have a problem with us. We're responsible corporate citizens with a heartfelt concern for the well-being of the communities we serve. We're the good guys!"

And sure enough, that's exactly how the personable 7-Eleven public relations man commenced our meeting. "Since 1976, as a national corporate sponsor of The Muscular Dystrophy Association, 7-Eleven has raised more than $25 million for research and patient care," Liles bragged. "We also raised more than $1 million last year for the March of Dimes' fight against birth defects." And while he was extolling 7-Eleven's good deeds, he made it a point to let me know they had "voluntarily" stopped selling cigarette paper because they had learned many customers were using it to roll marijuana joints. I responded the way I always do after a corporate representative tries to impress me by tooting his employer's horn. I expressed appreciation for 7-Eleven's philanthropic generosity on behalf of some fine causes. I also said I was glad to know of 7-Eleven's concern about America's growing drug use problem. But then I reminded him of the reason he had come to Tupelo. "Aren't you kind of robbing Peter to pay Paul?" I asked. "I mean, with one hand you're helping Jerry's kids. And that's great for the company image. "Yet, with the other hand," I continued, "in the name of corporate profits, you're a major contributor to America's huge child sexual abuse problem. I find that markedly hypocritical."

I don't remember exactly how Mr. Liles responded. However, I do remember that my comments didn't stop him from trying to convince me I should leave 7-Eleven alone. He felt if I was going to insist on making pornography sales an issue, I should pick on some of the other, "less responsible" convenience store chains. "We have a very restrictive policy for selling adult magazines," Liles said as he made his case. "In fact, our policy is usually much more stringent than local ordinances and serves as a model for the convenience store industry."

7-Eleven still wants to be the good guy

He then went on to explain in company-operated stores (approximately two-thirds of all 7-Eleven's nationwide), only *Playboy, Penthouse* and *Penthouse Forum* are available and approved for sale.

"They're kept behind the sales counter in a special rack that obstructs the covers from view," he emphasized. "We also prohibit their sale to minors under 18." Of course, Liles' wanted to convince me they had "voluntarily" taken all of these responsible measures in their effort to be, as one 7-Eleven newspaper ad said, "good neighbors."

But I wasn't convinced. Though Liles defended his company's enforcement procedures, I told him I knew their "Age 18" rule was frequently ignored in many parts of the country. Then I said, "I find it a bit unusual that a 'family store,' as you call it, sells items that can only be purchased by certain members of the family." As our conversation continued, I checked my watch to see how much time was left before church started. Though I thought his requested meeting time was a bit strange, Mr. Liles had explained that Sunday morning was the only time Southland's corporate jet was available.

So I had said I'd be happy to oblige him as long as he met me early before Sunday school and worship. With time running short, I mentioned one final reason why I felt 7-Eleven had no business pushing porno magazines. Early in my research of the sickening, perverted world of pornography, I discovered that *Playboy, Penthouse* and the more explicit publications frequently attack Christianity with a vengeance. So I showed Mr. Liles an eight-page section from a recent *Playboy* which happened to be titled, "*PRAYBOY:* Entertainment for Far Righteous Men."

Designed to look like a miniature issue of *Playboy,* the section is one of the most belittling, demeaning mockeries of Christians and the Christian faith I've ever seen. For example *PRAYBOY'S* cover features a photo of a nude Eve under an apple tree. Bold tasteless cover-blurbs such as "Girls of the Moral Majority: A Sensational Fully Clothed Pictorial" and "Christ Played Hurt: A Reverent Interview with Tom Landry" hype the contents inside.

The "Praymate of the Month" centerfold, "Mrs. December," is clad in a nightgown and pictured in her kitchen. One arm cradles a baby while the other holds up a scrub brush. Conspicuously visible behind her is a "Ten Commandments" plaque, a "Stand By Your Man" needlepoint sampler, an American flag and four books: *The Bible, Bible Stories, More Bible Stories* and *Still More Bible Stories.*

Also appearing with "Mrs. December" are her four older children. One of the girls carries an angel's harp. Indeed the picture's entire theme is one of ridicule and scorn for the home, the family, the country and Christianity. And that's only the beginning. Among a rather irreverent interview with "God" and a full-page advertisement for a "sin surveillance system" (a high-tech chastity belt) are plenty of blasphemous barbs making fun of Christ's words promising eternal life and his references to heaven.

After I finished reading some of the condescending copy from *PRAYBOY,* including a ridiculous letter that was not so subtly attributed to "J.C. II of Tupelo, Mississippi," I told Liles, "Your company sold more copies of this blasphemous mockery of heaven than anyone. Yet, your national advertising slogan is 'Thank heaven for 7-Eleven.' Don't you find that a bit ironic?

"I want no part of thanking heaven for 7-Eleven," I continued before he had a chance to answer. Then, intimating that the thought of a boycott had crossed my mind, I concluded, "I betcha there are millions more, who, just like me, might not want any part of it either." When I finished, Mr. Liles replied by noting that he was on a first name basis with both Hugh Hefner of *Playboy* and Bob Guccione, publisher of *Penthouse.* He even mentioned that he had been a guest at Hefner's famous mansion in Beverly Hills. Since "Hugh" and "Bob" did millions of dollars worth of business with 7-Eleven, Liles promised he would use his influence and "personally" see if he could get them to stop their constant Christian bashing.

7-Eleven will personally ask Hefner and Guccione to stop

As Liles did his name dropping, I smiled to myself. I knew he would only be wasting his time. Still, I figured it was about time Guccione and Hefner knew their days of unchallenged rosy relations with America's retail community were numbered. If our Sunday morning meeting had been a debate, I would have beaten the easy going 7-Eleven public relations professional hands down. I was interested in getting porn magazines out of some 7,500 7-Elevens. So when Mr. Liles called two months later and asked if I could meet him and the director of The National Convenience Store Association in Washington, D.C., I was more than happy to oblige.

Thinking that breakthrough with 7-Eleven was imminent, I flew to the nation's capital with a sense of expectancy. However, as the meeting began, I discovered 7-Eleven was holding fast to their position. In fact, as Allen Liles talked it seemed that nothing I had said during our previous Sunday morning rendezvous had registered. Still operating on the principle that 7-Eleven stores are the good guys, Liles proposed a plan to get the entire convenience store industry to adopt 7-Eleven's "strict adult magazine" sales policy. Of course, Liles thought I'd be pleased. After all, he said, his plan would make the more sexually explicit magazines (*Hustler, Chic, Swank, High Society,* etc.) being sold by many other major convenience store chains, less readily available.

"If you'll back our plan," Liles told me, "we'll use our influence to help make our policy the industry-wide standard." I listened intently until Liles finished. Then I once again made my position very clear. I told him I had no intention of supporting any plan enabling 7-Eleven to remain the world's number one porn pusher. "My intention," I emphasized, "is to get 7-Eleven to pull the magazines."

Our no-compromise angers 7-Eleven

As I spoke, I could tell Liles was flustered by my no-compromise attitude. In the corporate world, compromise is a way of life. Indeed, it's how most business deals are made. Most likely, when he learned his superiors at Southland had no intention of discontinuing *Playboy* and *Penthouse* sales, he worked overtime coming up with a deal he figured would get me off 7-Eleven's back. But now he had played his hand, and we were still locked in a stalemate.

At that point I knew, and I think Liles did too, it was useless to try to work out our differences behind the scenes. Still, a couple of months later on a hot July afternoon I once again found myself seated across from Allen Liles. This time it was on his turf in the office of Southland's President, Joe Thompson. A friend and AFA supporter who knew Joe personally had scheduled the appointment. He was certain if we could present our case face to face, Joe would "see the light" and pull the magazines. I had serious doubts, but went along anyway to see what the Southland president had to say.

Joe Thompson, who I guessed was about fifty, was friendly and politely listened while our mutual acquaintance quoted Scripture and appealed to our host's moral conscience – an approach I've found rarely works with most bottom-line oriented corporate CEO's. I hardly said a word. When the plea was over, Joe Thompson responded exactly the way I thought he would. "Our market research tells us customers who buy these magazines also tend to buy soda, potato chips, cigarettes... stuff like that," he said. "Pulling the magazines would cost us tens of millions of dollars."

Then he explained if 7-Eleven stopped selling porn and their competition didn't, they'd be handing business over to the other guys on a silver platter. "I appreciate your perspective," Joe Thompson concluded as he ushered us to the door. "But the magazines stay." Joe Thompson no doubt regretted his "our competitors all carry the magazines" argument a month or so later. That's when I learned the Chief Auto Parts chain, which is owned by Southland, stocked and sold the anti-Christian porn magazines. Some simple research revealed Chief was the only major auto parts chain in the country to do so.

My subsequent front page *AFA Journal* article pointing out this hypocrisy apparently embarrassed someone in Southland's corporate cathedral. Two weeks later all porn magazines were removed from Chief stores. Still, as Fall 1983 arrived the magazines were still being sold in 7-Eleven stores. Nevertheless I hadn't yet called for an official nationwide boycott against 7-Eleven. That's because, much to my disappointment, I had discovered most Christians and church leaders were oblivious both to pornography's destructiveness and its prevalence. And since I had never promoted a non-television boycott, I had some reservations about whether we could be successful.

I also had dragged my feet because, quite frankly, promoting consumer boycotts is not one of my favorite pastimes. Believe me, I can think of a thousand things I'd rather be doing instead of encouraging people not to buy "Brand X" or patronize "Store Y." If I could be faithful to my Lord by way of another calling I'd walk out of my office in a minute and never come back. But, to be responsible, I must press on. After all, how could I sleep at night if I didn't do something?

Putting the pressure on 7-Eleven

At any rate, on October 25, 1983, while I was still pondering whether or not to boycott 7-Eleven, I found myself standing on the stage at the Dallas Convention Center. People in the Dallas area had always been highly supportive of AFA's efforts to improve television. So we had organized a "Rally for Decency" there to generate additional enthusiasm.

Five thousand friendly folks had turned out for the rally. And after I showed several examples of anti-Christian programming on some giant screen TVs, I started talking about pornography. During my presentation, I pointed out he world's largest retailer of porn magazines was headquartered "right here in Dallas." With countless pornography victims in mind, I continued, "It's about time those of us who are sick and tired of what this trash is doing to America send 7-Eleven a message. I, for one, have not patronized a 7-Eleven since last January."

My comment was greeted by a loud crescendo of "Amens" and "Right Ons" mixed in with spontaneous applause. And that surprised me. But it was a good surprise. In fact, the approval coming from the audience seemed to trigger goose bumps from the top of my balding head to the tip of my toes. Completely disregarding my notes, I excitedly continued. "Will you join me by not going into a 7-Eleven?" As if on cue, the entire audience rose as one and their voices echoed in a chorus of agreement.

Since it was obvious they shared the deepest desire of my heart, I added, "Will you ask your friends not to buy from 7-Eleven?" And with that, the emotion reverberated with an ear-splitting roar. It sounded like the Cowboys had just scored the winning touchdown in the Super Bowl. I could hardly believe my ears and eyes. Here we were in downtown Dallas, only a stone's throw from the Southland/7-Eleven Corporate Center. Southland was one of the biggest employers in the city and respected as a pillar of the community. Yet, here were 5,000 Dallas area residents telling me they weren't going to spend one more dime at 7-Eleven until it pulled the porn.

At that moment, I realized I had heard the answer to my question. Yes, we were supposed to boycott 7-Eleven.

7-Eleven tries to ignore boycott

7-Eleven reacted to my subsequent official boycott announcement the same way the networks often do. They responded by not responding. Citizen complaints were almost completely ignored by Mr. Liles' staff.

And with the exception of a few memos designed to help individual store managers articulate the company line, 7-Eleven's national office tried to pretend the boycott didn't exist. The handful of 7-Eleven executives (mostly at regional offices) who did respond couldn't seem to understand what the fuss was all about. For instance, Bob Schiers, the 7-Eleven public relations director for New Jersey and Delaware, noted, "We don't think we're really doing anything wrong." John Pearman, South Florida division manager, seemed to be exasperated as to why Don Wildmon or anyone else would possibly have a beef with his fine employer. In his replies to complaint letters he proudly told how 7-Eleven President Jere W. Thompson (Joe Thompson's younger brother) had "personally seen to …" the removal of cigarette papers from 7-Eleven stores.

"This did affect the profit of the Southland Corporation," he explained. "But it was a conscientious decision we made because of the detriment it was having on the young people of our country." Then he added, "Thompson made this [decision] not only as a president of a large corporation, but also as a father of seven children."

I suppose some would commend Mr. Pearman for his corporate loyalty. But in light of my July meeting at 7-Eleven headquarters, I must say his letter elicited a good laugh. And about that time I needed a good laugh because I sensed our battle with 7-Eleven was going to be a lengthy campaign. Still, I wasn't discouraged because plenty of good news was coming from other fronts in the porn magazine war. Throughout the fall of 1983 I had been writing and calling top officials at many of the nation's smaller convenience store chains to explain our concerns. Most regional and national food and drug store chains had been contacted as well.

The walls begin to crumble

At the same time, I was strongly encouraging concerned citizens all over America to let their voices be heard. And soon our efforts, combined with the work of some other anti-pornography organizations, began to pay off. One hundred stores here, another one hundred stores there was paying off. During the winter of 1984, I got word of a minor victory almost every week. I was especially pleased in late January when I learned 190 Eckerd Drug Stores in their Dallas division pulled all their porn.

The seeds of triumph were planted when a Ft. Worth woman who had attended our Dallas rally showed some best-selling porn magazines to some friends. One of those friends happened to be the wife of a Dallas-area Eckerd Drug supervisor. She was shocked by the material's perversity and couldn't believe her husband's company was pandering it. Eventually, the "magazine issue" made its way through corporate bureaucratic channels. And in April it reached Eckerd Drug's founder and chairman, Jack Eckerd. Mr. Eckerd, who had recently made a serious Christian commitment (thanks in part to the witness of Chuck Colson), didn't even hesitate. He ordered the pornographic magazines out of all 1,000 of his stores.

I mention Eckerd because they were the first major player in the porn retailing scene to take an anti-porn stand. And I believed Eckerd's action might help influence some other large national chains to stop selling porn. As soon as I heard of Eckerd's decision, I called Allen Liles and asked if 7-Eleven planned to follow suit. When he said no, I decided it was time to increase our pressure. So I scheduled our first nationwide picketing of 7-Eleven stores for August 6.

I was convinced we needed to get tougher with 7-Eleven when I learned an eight-month-old St. Petersburg, Florida, girl had died while she was being sexually assaulted by two boys, ages seven and nine. According to testimony at the trial, while the babysitter was in another room, the two boys looked at some of their mother's sex magazines (not all porn addicts are men). They mimicked what they had seen.

Picketing in hundreds of 7- Eleven cities

When August 6 arrived, I'm pleased to say faithful friends jointly walked the picket lines at 560 7-Eleven stores in 168 cities (according to figures based upon written reports mailed in by our volunteer picketing coordinator in each city). We also picketed scores of other porn-selling stores in cities without a 7-Eleven. To our knowledge, it was the most massive picketing of its kind in history. Yet, true to their strategy of pretending, we boycotters didn't exist. 7-Eleven officials did all they could to deny our impact. For instance, Doug Reed, 7-Eleven's media relations director, told the press "his office had received spotty reports of protesting in a few areas of the country, but nothing substantial."

"We put it in the category of not being a big deal," added 7-Eleven regional manager, Fred Davis. But contrary to their no-big-deal public façade, I knew our effort was "an issue of great concern to Southland." That's a direct quote from a memo written by Kent Young of Southland's Dallas Corporate Office. He then warned the approximately 40 managers who received the memo that things, "will become more heated as Rev. Wildmon tries to put more pressure on the company." A copy of this memo arrived in my mail the same way just about every other 7-Eleven in-house directive detailing the company's boycott battling plans did. It was sent by one of the thousands of Southland 7-Eleven employees who were on our side.

Since they couldn't officially support the boycott, many realized they could help by unofficially supplying "the enemy" with inside information. Therefore, I knew just about every countermove 7-Eleven was going to make before they made it. These inside sources let me know we were "putting a dent in the wall of 7-Eleven's pornography sales," as one high-level supervisor, who requested anonymity, wrote. "These responses [memos] from our division merchandizing department let me know the scuttle in the air is working," he added shortly after our August 6 picket. "I would not continue to work here if I didn't see some light in this issue." Since I knew we were having an impact, I scheduled and announced three more national 7-Eleven pickets for October, January and April. I figured if we could keep turning the screw, sooner or later Joe Thompson would wise up and say, "Hey, the best thing to do is to get out of this mess because it's just going to keep getting bigger and bigger."

Picketing in front of 600 7-Eleven stores

In October sign-carrying friends demonstrated at more than 600 stores. And in January, our numbers were remarkably good considering the circumstances. Being a warm-blooded Southerner, I had forgotten how cold it sometimes gets in the Dakotas, Minnesota, Michigan and upstate New York. And wouldn't you know it, on the day of our picket, temperatures throughout the Midwest plunged far below zero. Wind chills, which ranged anywhere from -50 to -90 degrees, only made things worse.

Brrrrrr!

Nevertheless, thousands of hearty, faithful souls braved the elements to let the Southland Corporation know their porn-pushing outlets did not "enhance and improve the quality of life" as the 7-Eleven promotional brochure "Your Neighborhood Store" claimed. Larry Johnson, our volunteer picketing coordinator in Cedar Rapids, Iowa, told me that despite a -80 degree wind chill, they had 125 people picketing nine 7-Elevens. Then he proudly said, "We only had one case of slight frost bite."

"We'll help whenever you say go," added George DeLong of Beaver Crossing, Nebraska, as he indicated how "pleased" he was with their turnout. The "16 below zero" temperature reading, he said, only seemed to make it more of an adventure for everyone, an adventure including plenty of steaming hot chocolate.

One 7-Eleven manager does the right thing

As I poured over the January picketing reports, one non-weather related comment in particular caught my eye. I read how our protestors in Lincoln Park, Michigan, had been pleasantly surprised when the 7-Eleven manager, at the risk of being fired, removed the magazines. Then he put on his jacket and joined them. He even carried a sign for awhile.

Similar occurrences had happened several times before, but this incident had special meaning. This manager had witnessed firsthand the destruction caused by sexual deviancy. You see, the previous spring I received a letter describing a brutal rape and beating in the back room of a Lincoln Park, Michigan, 7-Eleven. The rapist was none other than a 7-Eleven clerk.

Thinking the girl who was raped was dead, the attacker put her in a garbage bag and threw her in the back of his pickup. But she revived and escaped while he finished working his shift. The letter, which was also sent to 7-Eleven officials in Dallas, was written by a Lincoln Park man who had spoken with police and the girl's mother at the hospital. Three months later, in April, we picketed almost 1,000 stores, 700 of them owned or franchised by the Southland Corporation. Still, the Thompson brothers (Joe's older brother, John, serves as Southland's Chairman) weren't giving in. This was despite the fact some 7,000 stores (600 Super X drug stores, 400 Super America gas stations, 450 Albertsons food stores, etc.), including hundreds of independently owned, franchised 7-Elevens, had stopped selling porn magazines during the past year.

Then, during the summer of 1985, two things happened that made me realize I just might have to try to embarrass the Thompson brothers into pulling the porn. First, I learned the Southland Corporation had given a $250,000 grant for child abuse awareness and prevention. To add insult to injury, Southland bragged that this was the largest corporately-funded effort of its kind ever undertaken in this country. Second, at the same time, the music star Madonna appeared in various stages of undress in both *Playboy* and *Hustler*. Referring to Madonna's porn magazine debut, Dr. Judith Reisman, who was just finishing an in-depth study on "Images of Children, Crime and Violence in *Playboy*, *Penthouse* and *Hustler* magazines," concluded many children would now be more easily victimized by child pornographers since the youngsters would be urged to simply do what their idol Madonna had done.

Dr. Reisman's study plays important role

Dr. Reisman's study, prepared for the office of Juvenile Justice and Delinquency Prevention at the U.S. Justice Department, discussed how the photographs, illustrations and cartoons depicting children in these magazines (*Playboy*, 8.2 times per issue; *Penthouse*, 6.4 times per issue) make "children more acceptable as objects of abuse, neglect and mistreatment, especially sexual abuse and exploitation." With Southland's ridiculous double standard in mind, I decided to hold a March Against Pornography in Dallas, Texas, on Labor Day morning, 1985. Labor Day, of course, is when Jerry Lewis holds his annual Telethon for Muscular Dystrophy.

Some 13,000 concerned citizens (by official police estimate) turned out for our rally in Cole Park which featured short speeches by Jerry Falwell, Tim and Beverly LaHaye, and several other nationally known evangelists, pastors and Christian leaders who had flown in for the occasion. Then, all 13,000 "porn busters," as some of the press called us, made the three-quarter-mile trek through the streets of Dallas to the Southland/7-Eleven Corporate headquarters.

Indeed at the very moment Jerry Lewis was trumpeting 7-Eleven's corporate generosity, we were holding hands, singing hymns and chorusing "Don't Thank Heaven for 7-Eleven." To our knowledge, it was the largest anti-pornography event ever held, anywhere! Though virtually ignored nationally, our Dallas rally and march was covered extensively by the local media. And as I found out later from our strategically-placed friends, the Thompsons were plenty embarrassed. I also learned, again from my well-positioned inside sources, that 7-Eleven was really starting to feel our boycott where it counts. In the pocketbook, of course.

That fall, *Advertising Age* reported porn sales were worth about "$30 million" a year to 7-Eleven. Yet, enough people had taken their business elsewhere to more than offset 7-Eleven's profits from porn peddling. The problem was, 7-Eleven knew if they pulled the magazines right away it would look like they had knuckled under to Wildmon and his, to quote Hugh Hefner, "evangelical terrorists." They needed a reason, any reason, that would allow them to get out of the porn business while saving their corporate pride.

That "reason" finally came in April 1986 in the form of The Meese Commission Report on Pornography. After announcing 7-Eleven would no longer sell adult magazines in their 4,500 corporately-owned and run stores, 7-Eleven president Jere W. Thompson explained, "The testimony [of the Meese Commission] indicates a growing public awareness of a possible connection between adult magazines and crime, violence and child abuse."

7-Eleven's action started a chain reaction. During the next few weeks, 5,000 more stores pulled their porn, including 2,000 Revco drug stores and 1,400 Rite Aid "family" drug stores. I was especially thrilled with Rite Aid's wise decision. Rite Aid's chairman, Alex Grass, had once called us "rabble rousers" as he defended films like **Daddy's Little Girls**, **The Younger the Better**, **Bodies in Heat** and **Desires Within Young Girls** which appeared in his company's video catalog. I wonder if my "you're next" letter had anything to do with his change of heart?

At any rate, thanks in large measure to 7-Eleven's action, the two-year total of porn pulling stores passed 20,000. As I contemplated this, I knew much of the credit needed to go to the 18,000 folks who attended our two Dallas rallies and the 100,000 people who directly contacted 7-Eleven by phone or letter. I also knew I owed a special word of thanks to each faithful friend who had carried a picket sign in scorching heat and bone-chilling cold. You know, the folks Hugh Hefner had angrily called "literary death squads." Of course, I could certainly understand why Mr. Hefner was so agitated. In the months immediately following 7-Eleven's action, Playboy's circulation dropped 23 percent, an average of 674,000 copies per month.

We gave thanks to God for this major victory, and to those thousands who joined in taking a stand for righteousness.

31

Mighty Mouse and Garbage Pail Kids move to the front

Dear Ann Landers:

In February you printed a letter about a toddler in Boston who was stabbed seventeen times by a five-year-old. You said the child probably got the idea from watching TV. Well, let me suggest another possibility. I shall do my best to tone my letter down because the words to describe this filth cannot be printed in a family newspaper.

This trash is called Garbage Pail Kids, published by Topps Chewing Gum Company. These cards are obtained when the kids buy gum. They are traded back and forth and the idea is to get a big collection.

I shall try to describe some of the cards I'm looking at. One is a colored drawing of a child who has been stabbed in the back and his head has been split open with an axe. The blood is gushing out. Another card shows a child who has been run over and crushed by a car. Still another pictures a little boy with fourteen spikes going through his body.

The most disturbing card pictures a child grinning after he shoots a little girl. The dead child is lying on the ground with three bullet holes in her body. The boy is laughing.

Our eight-year-old neighbor boy has a Garbage Pail poster that shows an infant stabbed with knives, hypodermic needles and swords. The infant is wearing a target. The caption on the poster says, "Have a Nice Day."

At a time when so many children are being abused we do not need this kind of trash that pictures children as garbage. Please use the power of your column to alert parents to this monstrous thing.

Ellen H. in Houston, Texas

Dear Ellen:

I wrote about Garbage Pail Kids a few years ago and was under the impression that we had gotten rid of them. Apparently we haven't.

I urge all parents to refuse to patronize drugstores, grocery stores, candy stores or novelty shops where these cards are offered. Tell the manager why you won't be coming in any more.

If your child has these cards, take them away and explain why they are bad to have. Make it plain that hurting and killing people is not funny and that nobody should joke about violence and murder.

Ann Landers

© Ann Landers, Creators/Los Angeles Times Syndicates. Reprinted by Permission.

Garbage In: Garbage Out!

America's favorite advice columnist is right! Garbage Pail Kids cards, produced and marketed by Topps, the company famous for its baseball cards, truly are a "monstrous thing," as Houston's Ellen H. asserts. But, the shocking children's trading cards she described in her letter to Ann Landers only scratch the surface of Garbage Pail Kids nightmare.

Other cards depict "Busted Bob," a baby boy whose severed arms and legs are scattered across the floor and "Well Done Sheldon," who has been roasted to order at the stake. Toddler "Nerdy Norm" smokes four cigarettes at once. "Boozin' Bruce" is an infant wino clutching a liquor-filled baby bottle. And these are only a few of the revolting characters that were available.

Within days after these bizarre collectibles featuring murder, brutality, self-abuse, sadistic torture, rebellion, anarchy, cannibalism and even child suicide first hit store shelves in 1985, I began getting phone calls and letters from exasperated parents. "What's this world coming to?"

many asked. Then they'd tell me how their children, just like many of their friends, had blown their entire allowance on the grotesque cards.

Indeed, the cards were tremendously popular. For a couple of years, Garbage Pail Kids collecting obsessed millions of young people. In 1986, Topps spokesman Norman Liss revealed that, "The demand is incredible. More than we can keep with," And that's what broke the hearts of the parents who contacted me.

Since children are only beginning to learn how to differentiate between right and wrong, good and evil, these parents believed that frequent exposure to these diabolical images couldn't be anything but harmful. Simple logic told them that children who see deranged behavior portrayed as humorous and cute will be more likely to accept abnormal behavior as normal. Realizing that an entire generation was being weaned on this appropriately named "Garbage," these parents were furious.

Many state PTA organizations, such as New Jersey's, called the cards "psychologically harmful" and begged Topps to stop making them and stores to stop selling them. Scores of psychologists who feared that some children would act out what they had seen joined the crusade as well.

Unfortunately Topps Chairman Arthur T. Shorin apparently determined right and wrong on the basis of profits. His public relations people pointed out the "enormous popularity" of his torrid card series, as if that somehow justified its existence. Then, inferring that Garbage Pail Kids critics didn't know what they were talking about, Topps officials repeatedly stated, "We wouldn't put them out if we thought they were wrong." They also had vowed to keep "marketing them as long as parents keep buying them."

I countered Topps' self-serving rationalization by urging everyone to do what Ann Landers recommended: Boycott stores that sell Garbage Pail Kids. I also reproduced some actual cards in our monthly Journal so people could see for themselves how blatantly abusive they were.

But, with so many of my organization's resources tied up in pressuring pornography pushers, I didn't make battling Garbage Pail Kids a top priority. However, that policy changed instantaneously one sweltering July day in 1987.

I had been browsing through one of the entertainment industry trade journals when I stumbled across some shocking, but not surprising, news. I learned Judy Price, CBS vice president of children's programming, had purchased the television rights for these abominable characters that promote demonically based behavioral change. CBS planned to headline its new fall Saturday morning line-up with **Garbage Pail Kids**, the cartoon show.

That's right! Come September 19, millions of little ones would get to see creepy, make-believe characters such as "Bustin' Dustin" (a baby boxer with perpetual nosebleed) and "Basket Casey" (a boy who dribbles his own severed head like a basketball) magically come to animated life. Through various sources I learned that the animated children on the Garbage Pail Kids show would first appear as if they were normal. But by uttering the mantra "Trash Out," they could magically assume the identity of a grotesque Garbage Pail Kids character.

Of course, Judy Price claimed the program would be harmless. She promised that no television character would cut off his own head, poke her own eyes out, set off firecrackers in his mouth or stuff herself into a trash compactor, as some of the card characters do.

But as far as I was concerned, CBS had stooped lower than they ever had before to make a dollar. I agreed with my friend, Dr. Thomas Radecki of The National Coalition on Television Violence, when he said, "By using anything related to the cards, they're saying it's okay to get a laugh out of brutal sadism."

Time was short. Still, I was determined to mobilize a large protest against CBS. In the process, I hoped that hard-hearted CBS officials would be so overwhelmed with anti-Garbage Pail Kids sentiment that, for once, they'd sit up and take notice.

As I thought of the sick, slick message a Garbage Pail Kids cartoon show would send to young ones all across the land, I was mighty glad I could count on more concerned friends than ever before to stand with me. Direct support for my organization (The American Family Association) had multiplied many times during the 1980's. That enabled me to challenge and inform 325,000 individuals, couples, pastors and churches through the monthly American Family Association (AFA) *Journal*. In fact, almost half the pastors and churches in America received timely updates.

The days when people had kidded me about being the Lone Ranger from Tupelo were ancient history. Now I had plenty of high-skilled riders in the storm. This increased support also helped the American Family Association significantly expand its overall outreach.

For instance, we were able to hire a national director for our 400 AFA Chapters located in almost all 50 states. Made up of citizen volunteers, these groups primarily focused on ridding their communities of pornography and porn-related businesses.

To better support our AFA Chapters, we also added a legal department. Believe me, when you do battle with the well-financed and highly-organized pornographers, you need all the legal expertise you can get.

Four thousand volunteer monitors helped us keep close tabs on prime-time network programming and sponsors each fall and spring. Someone else had taken over responsibility for coordinating that effort. Another AFA staff member helped with the extensive research and preparation necessary for my daily Don Wildmon Report radio broadcast aired on some 200 stations nationwide.

At any rate, in addition to publicizing my Garbage Pail Kids protest in the *AFA Journal* and on my radio show, I mailed out 620,000 individual letters to people I believed would take action. The response was incredible. During late August and early September, CBS was bombarded with cards, letters and phone calls from flabbergasted adults. Their message: Trash the show.

But it wasn't only grown-ups who let CBS know their feelings. Some kids were disgusted, too. After signing and sending a protest card to

CBS, nine-year-old Chad Birdwell of Kingsville, Texas, sent me part of his allowance to assist our effort. He explained that he thought the cards "were sickening and a very bad influence," especially the ones that "suggest suicide."

"After Dad told me what your letter was about, I was happy to know that there are some adults out there willing to help us kids," Chad wrote. "Thanks for trying to clean up America for us kids."

Needless to say, touching testimonials like Chad's gave me plenty of incentive to personally contact every potential Garbage Pail Kids adviser I could think of. My request was very simple: Please don't help pay for CBS's "Garbage." Then, after warning them of probably economic repercussions if they sponsored the show, I explained why so many people did not want to see the Garbage Pail Kids on TV.

Normally when I write or call about a yet-to-be-aired program, only a handful of sponsors will take the time to send a "we agree with you, we won't be on the show" response. However, I knew CBS's Garbage Pail Kids plans had shocked officials at many of America's major corporations that advertise on children's programs when what seemed like almost every company on my list responded. Not only did they tell me they wouldn't be buying Garbage Pail Kids commercial time, but also most said they wouldn't appear on the show even if CBS gave the time away.

As a result, on September 15, four days before the scheduled Garbage Pail Kids premier, CBS quietly announced that they were canceling the show. The dearth of willing advertisers, combined with the intense public protest, had forced CBS executives to eat their $3 million Garbage pail Kids investment (almost a dozen episodes were already completed).

The next day *Variety* reported "nobody at CBS wanted to comment on the abrupt tossing out of its 'Garbage.' However, "insiders admitted the move was due to demands by various pressure groups not to air the series."

Since the American Family Association was the only group the article specifically mentioned, I recognized that I was reading about a great victory. It was a victory that ultimately belonged to both the children of America and the Lord of heaven whose love for little ones is immeasurable. Faithful friends like young Chad Birdwell had helped make television history. To my knowledge, this was the first time a network had ever announced a decision to air a series and then canceled that series because of public outrage.

As I reflected on CBS's historic action, I chuckled as I recalled some defiant words spoken by CBS Broadcast Group president Gene Jankowski. "CBS will never cave into Wildmon's demands," he had promised after my duel with Gene Mater six years earlier. "To do so would be tantamount to betraying our own principles."

"We are clearly dealing with principles here, not money," Jankowski proudly continued. "No show will be canceled from CBS because of pressure of this type, regardless of sponsorship or no sponsorship."

I hope I'm not guilty of the same stubborn pride when I admit it felt kind of good to see my longtime network nemesis "betray his principles." Still, I had learned enough about CBS to know that sooner or later some high level executive would look at the $3 million and try and resurrect the show. I was especially concerned when I discovered that Judy Price was lobbying hard behind the scenes to get Jankowski and her other bosses to reverse their decision. "It ain't over until the fat lady sings," she told the Los Angeles Times.

A few months later I got a tip that CBS was considering sneaking Garbage Pail Kids into the schedule before another protest could be mounted. So I was left with no choice but to ask AFA friends to hit CBS with another round of cards, letters and phone calls. I also had people implore CBS not to sell the completed episodes to a cable network or a children's programming syndication service.

Unfortunately that's exactly what CBS finally did. CBS dumped the video version of this trash, no doubt at a fire-sale price, on The Movie Channel (TMC), a pay cable network. To our knowledge, the series has never been shown on any network channel.

At any rate, even though CBS ultimately did not air *Garbage Pail Kids*, Judy Price's children's division was still tossing plenty of junk onto the trash heap of mind-polluting television programming. Let me elaborate ...

CBS Deals Dope on Saturday Morning

One May 1988 morning I found myself standing next to several American Family Association staff members in our video recording room. That's where we kept about a half-dozen videocassette recorders and televisions sets.

In the early 1980's, AFA videotaped virtually all evening prime-time programming (365 days a year) aired on ABC, CBS and NBC. That way, when the networks ridiculed Christianity or presented uncalled for violence or gratuitous sex, we had the evidence in living color. However, on this particular occasion, we weren't watching a program we had taped ourselves. Instead we were all watching a Saturday morning cartoon, recorded by a Kentucky mother while she was out shopping with her kids.

This woman had phoned our office a few days earlier. And to be honest, I thought she was just another crank caller trying to play a practical joke on us. The incredible charge she made against CBS was so ludicrous, I found it impossible to believe. Sensing I thought she was off base, she offered to send me her video tape so I could see for myself.

As the tape she sent rolled, I focused my eyes on a furry little mouse with big ears and a cape. The animated rodent, who was depressed because the lady mouse he loved had not been responding to his affection, was reclining next to a campfire at the end of a long day. A few moments later the melancholy mouse reached under his cape and pulled out a powdery looking substance. Then I noticed the powder suddenly disappeared right up the creature's nose.

"Please tell me I didn't actually see what I think I just saw," I said to my co-workers, who appeared to be in a state of shock. "Let's see that again."

When the tape rewound, we again watched the TV screen in incredulous wonder as the scenario repeated itself. Into the cape went the cartoon character's hand. Out came a powdery substance. Up his nose it went.

"Our Kentucky friend wasn't kidding," I finally said, breaking the sober silence in the room. "It's as plain as day. They've really got Mighty Mouse snorting cocaine."

I was especially outraged because in the next scene Mighty Mouse's depression had lifted and he was his usual, heroic self. Though I doubted if any children watching the Saturday morning show were cognizant of the subliminal message, I sure didn't miss it: Need a lift? Just take some cocaine. It's the perfect pick-me-up.

Later that day, to make absolutely certain our eyes weren't playing tricks on us, we invited two agents from The Mississippi Bureau of Narcotics to our Tupelo office. Without telling them what to watch for, we showed them the taped episode. Their response: "There's no question. Mighty Mouse is snorting coke."

During the next several days I tried to figure out how and why CBS could have allowed the unthinkable on a cartoon show viewed by millions of children. And the more I thought, the more I realized my questions weren't all that difficult to answer.

First, I remembered a two-part series about cocaine use in Hollywood which appeared in *TV Guide* magazine back in the early 80's. "Cocaine is so popular in the world of Hollywood television studios, it sometimes is used to pay producers, performers and writers," the nation's most-read TV publication had reported. The previous year (1987), The Associated Press had quoted Tom Kenny, director of a Hollywood substance abuse counseling center called Studio 12. Drugs in the movie and television business are "out of control," said Kenny. "Cocaine is the prime culprit."

Second, I turned my attention specifically to **Mighty Mouse: The New Adventures**, which the latest issue of *TV Guide's* message to parents continued, "If you're not joining the kids on the couch Saturday mornings, you're missing something. That's for sure, I thought to myself.

But when *TV Guide* said the new "refashioned" CBS cartoon hero was produced and animated by none other than Ralph Bakshi of **Fritz the Cat** fame, all kinds of red flags went up inside my mind. You see, when I had of necessity familiarized myself with the pornography business I'd learned that **Fritz the Cat**, bankrolled in part by Hugh Hefner, made history as the first X-rated animated feature film. Knowing that CBS had hired a notorious pornographer to create the new children's hero, I decided I'd better check out the man behind the mouse. And it didn't take long to find out that Ralph Bakshi is no Walt Disney.

To my dismay, I discovered that sex, violence and drugs are major sub-themes in most of Bakshi's X- and R-rated feature films such as **Heavy Traffic**, **American Pop** and **Coonskin. Fritz the Cat**, for example, features a marijuana-smoking orgy. Bakshi's imagery becomes more understandable when one learns he grew up in the New York City ghetto where the neighborhood gang called themselves "The Hell-Bent Rapists." Referring in part to his claim to have been "accidentally splattered by blood from a Mafioso hit" at age eight, the New York Times once concluded, "At bottom, Bakshi is well aware that his scarred upbringing will underlie everything he does in films."

"I work a stream of consciousness, recalling events from my whole life," Bakshi told the Times. "I go all out to express my hostilities." That comment especially made sense when I learned that the National Coalition on Television Violence had ranked **Mighty Mouse: The New Adventures** the most violent program aired on Saturday mornings, featuring some sixty violent acts per hour.

After I had studied Bakshi's revealing bio, the third and final piece of the Mighty Mouse cocaine-snorting puzzle fell into place. I remembered some comments made one year earlier by CBS vice president for children's programming, Judy "Garbage Pail Kids" Price. In a Los Angeles Times interview, Price explained the surprising reason why she had entered the field of children's programming. "I could get away with more, which is strange, isn't it?" she bragged. Noting that she could get more "controversial subject matter" past the network censors, she continued, "I think we've broken a lot of ground where people would not have dared to go in prime time."

In the midst of the Garbage Pail fight I had indirectly asked Price if that series was what she meant by "breaking new ground" and "getting away with more." Now I wondered if Mighty Mouse epitomized what she had been talking about.

Of course, Price never answered my question relating to her "breaking new ground" and "getting away with more" statements. Instead she repeatedly denied making them. I got a kick out of her mendacious response, however, because the Los Angeles Times interviewer confirmed that Price had actually reviewed and approved the completed article before it went to press.

I decided that there was absolutely no way I was going to let Judy Price and her employer get away with sending a pro-drug message to America's children. So I had several hundred black and white still photographs reproduced from the actual video. Then on Saturday, June 4, 1988, with the pictured evidence enclosed, I mailed an exposé-type press release to newspapers and magazines all over America.

Anatomy of a CBS Cover-up

On Monday June 6, pandemonium broke out at CBS headquarters. Journalists bombarded CBS with Mighty Mouse-related inquiries. And panic-stricken CBS officials, caught completely by surprise, didn't have the foggiest idea of how to respond. Finally, by mid-afternoon, CBS had changed their "no comment" to "we'll release a prepared statement tomorrow [Tuesday] afternoon."

Hurriedly, CBS vice president for program practices, George Dessart, prepared a response indicating "CBS categorically denies that Mighty Mouse or any other character was shown sniffing cocaine." It included a bizarre explanation that Mighty Mouse was, in reality, "enjoying the smell of his 'lucky chunk of cheese.'"

How is it possible to grate a "lucky chunk of cheese" into a fine powder and then snort it, I'll never know. But apparently, at first that's what CBS wanted me and millions of Americans to believe. I say "at first" because I wasn't supposed to receive Dessart's "lucky chunk of cheese" letter, dated June 7, 1988.

You see, CBS had remained silent much too long. So when Tuesday afternoon arrived, several reporters were begging them to make good on their promise to issue a prepared statement. Consequently George Dessart foolishly faxed a few copies to a handful of anxious reporters as soon as it was ready. Of course, he had no way of knowing that one of those reporters happened to be a friend of mine. And that meant I had his letter in my hands within minutes.

Later that day, prior to final mail call, CBS discovered they had a problem. Though they weren't talking to reporters, Ralph Bakshi was. Naturally, he was absolutely livid, calling my charges "lunacy." Then, sounding a lot like Lee Rich, Gene Mater and other Don Wildmon bashers, he said the whole affair "smacks of burning books and the Third Reich." However, CBS's trouble stemmed from the fact that Bakshi never mentioned any "lucky chunk of cheese." Instead, he claimed the substance disappearing up Mighty Mouse's nose was a handful of – get this – "crushed flowers."

Imagine my surprise when I discovered that George Dessart had quickly changed his story to match Bakshi's. In my "official" letter, dated June 8, Dessart told me I had actually seen Mighty Mouse sniffing the "aroma" from a "mass of crushed stems, tomatoes and flowers."

Dessart's letter, which was also released to the media at large, is the most deceptive letter I've seen written by a major network official. He called my "flight of fancy" an "irresponsible misrepresentation" which takes "three seconds of airtime [actually, it's about six seconds] out of context."

Sadly, much of the media around the nation believed Dessart's lies.

Not knowing the truth, officials at the Texarkana Gazette wrote an editorial representative of many. Labeling me a "zealot reactionary trying to make a name for himself," they said. "Frankly, we think Wildmon is full of himself. If the Mouse's creator, Ralph Bakshi, or CBS, committed any sins, it was in having the dignity to respond to such lame attacks."

I guess I can't really blame the editorial staff at the Texarkana Gazette for blindly siding with CBS. I had found the thought of Mighty Mouse snorting coke difficult to believe at first. At the same time, most of the good folks on America's Main Streets did not know that CBS, proving they indeed had something to hide, was not honoring requests for the video footage. Most major television advertisers, radio stations, newspapers and even ABC and NBC television stations had to get their copies of the actual coke-snorting scene from me.

Shortly after the initial Mighty Mouse Media furor died down, I was startled to learn I had not been the first concerned individual to alert CBS to this travesty. That dubious honor went to Dino Corbin, general manager of the CBS television affiliate, KHSL, in Chico, California.

Like me, Mr. Corbin had been highly skeptical when a viewer said that her 6-and 10-year-old children had seen "Mighty Mouse snort coke." But when Mr. Corbin reviewed the tape, like me, he became a believer. Before he contacted Judy Price, he showed the episode, called "The Littlest Tramp," to eight station employees. To a person they all said, "Mighty Mouse is doing a line." That is slang for snorting cocaine.

But most startling of all, Dino Corbin had alerted CBS to Mighty Mouse's drug habit the previous December. That's right! The videotape I saw was not the first time CBS aired the cartoon, but the third.

Even more startling was the fact that CBS officials had assured Corbin in December that the scene would be cut. Yet they did nothing. It made me wonder if some high ranking CBS executives were deliberately trying to poison the minds of our young people by teaching them it's okay to use drugs.

By late June, I was sick and tired of CBS's obvious conspiracy to cover up the truth about their cartoon mouse. Not only had they deceived the American public with a whole series of distorted lies, they had done it so craftily that most people believed that Don Wildmon was the villain. As I prayed about additional ways to bring the truth to light, I remembered an offer George Dessart made in his deceitful June 8 letter.

"We would be happy to show you or your associates the episode of **Mighty Mouse: The New Adventures** which was broadcast over the CBS Television Network on April 23, 1988," "he had written. "It would appear that you have not had the opportunity since what is described in your press release bears no relation to anything CBS has broadcast or would consider broadcasting."

Of course, George Dessart knew I had seen the episode. He had cunningly made and worded his offer so that the nation's journalists would think Don Wildmon had completely lost touch with reality. I don't think he ever, for a moment, thought I'd actually take him up on it. But that's what I felt led to do.

Since Tupelo doesn't have a CBS affiliate station, I called Dessart and asked if I could see the episode while I was in Washington, D.C., on some other business. He couldn't very well renege on his offer. So once the arrangements were made, I invited all 535 U.S. congresspersons and senators to the special screening. I also invited several members of the national press corps.

When show time arrived, so did more than two dozen congressional staff members, including aides to Senator Helms of North Carolina and Representatives Bliley of Virginia, Chandler of Washington and Dannemeyer of California. When reporters such as Bill Anderson of United Press International began appearing, the CBS employee in charge excused herself, I assumed, so she could call New York. The moment she returned she told the members of the press to leave. However, when I pointed out that would appear to be an obvious admission of guilt, she eventually let everyone enter the screening room.

When it was over, I could tell that everyone was horrified that Mighty

Mouse had taken drugs and were so angered that CBS had so brazenly lied to the American people.

The next day Congressman Rod Chandler expressed his "utter outrage" to CBS president Laurence Tisch. After describing his skepticism at what "simply had to be a crazy accusation," Chandler told Tisch he had dispatched two attorneys from his staff to the screening.

"They both concluded, after viewing the entire program once and the scene in question several times, that the only conclusion that could be reached is that Mighty Mouse indeed had snorted cocaine," Congressman Chandler wrote. "Frankly the response of CBS has been completely inadequate. That the powder in question was a 'mass of crushed stems, tomatoes and flowers which the character was smelling in typical cartoon fashion,' is unbelievable to anyone who has seen the program.

"In view of the drug crisis facing this country and the need to educate our children on the dangers of drugs," Chandler continued, "airing this program was unforgivable. The fact that CBS has refused to admit its mistake or to act to prevent this kind of mistake in the future is equally unforgivable."

So outraged was the Washington congressman, and rightfully so, that he sent a copy of this letter, along with still pictures of the coke-snorting scene, to every one of his colleagues on Capitol Hill.

But it wasn't just public servants who got angry at CBS. So did many big-time advertisers, including Ralston Purina and Mars, Incorporated who both had unsuspectingly pushed products on the infamous coke-snorting show.

Ralston chose to take a low key approach and simply told CBS they, "in all candor, share the concerns of the critics." Mars, on the other hand, wrote the most condemnatory letter I had ever seen from a sponsor address to a network. CBS certainly didn't help their cause by making Mars beg, time and time again, for a copy of the episode.

After he finally had seen it, Mars vice president Edward J. Stegemann told Laurence Tisch that he had been directed by Mars stockholders to "express their outrage." "This appears to be one of the most irresponsible and unprofessional examples of network programming we have ever heard about," Stegemann said. Then he explained Mars first learned about "this outrageous episode" when they were "deluged" by consumer complaints.

"We're dumbfounded that something like this could have taken place," Stegemann continued, "and once taken place, to be so terribly mishandled by one of the country's major communication companies. We believe that CBS owes the public an apology for airing so reprehensible an episode.

"The fact that it appeared during 'children's time' on Saturday morning," he added, "just magnifies the misconduct."

Still, despite the justifiable clamor for a public apology from individuals, the Texarkana Gazette could hardly label "zealot reactionaries," CBS never once intimated wrongdoing on their part. As usual, they arrogantly abrogated all responsibility, confident the whole matter would quietly fade away.

Oh sure, CBS finally did cut the coke snorting sequence from the episode. It took Congressman Chandler's forceful letter to get them to do that. Laurence Tisch also fired George Dessart soon after he received the letter from Mars, Incorporated. Though I hoped Tisch would fire Dessart for being deceptive, I'm afraid he was fired for not being deceptive enough (i.e., the "lucky chunk of cheese" escapade and allowing the Washington, D.C. screening).

CBS never disciplined Judy Price, and waited a year before firing Ralph Baksi.

32

Columnist says Don is right

Ron Alridge wrote of me: "A country boy with right on his side." Alridge was a TV-radio critic for the Chicago Tribune. This article appeared in the October, 1, 1981 edition.

I was utterly surprised when this column ran in the liberal Chicago Tribune. It is the one in a thousand columns.

Here is the column.

The Rev. Don Wildmon just won't go away. The conservative United Methodist minister from Tupelo, Mississippi, who heads the National Federation for Decency has been ridiculed; ignored, and publicly debated, but somehow he always lands on his feet.

The latest survival exercise came this week. When Wildmon appeared on the popular Phil Donahue's nationally syndicated talk show, which the minister's TV-monitoring group has attacked as too sexy. The taped show was broadcast Tuesday in Chicago, where Donahue is based, and will be shown nationally soon. The show is carried by 222 stations.

An unusually large Donahue audience was on hand for the taping, mainly because it occurred in Salt Lake City, where fans don't routinely get a chance to be in the audience and where the arena is larger than the show's regular studio in Chicago.

Donahue introduced Wildmon politely, urging the audience to make him feel welcome. Wildmon, wading through the applauding crowd to take his place alongside the host, appeared slightly nervous and drawled that he must be crazy to publicly debate such a talented foe. It was the same technique the country slick preacher used to cast himself as the underdog at the outset of last June's debate with CBS vice president Gene Mater. Wildmon won that debate – decisively.

This time there was no clear winner, though. Wildmon probably gained the most points simply because he didn't fall on his face. Donahue was firm, but fair.

Wildmon was sincere and gentlemanly. Donahue argued that discussing sexual topics on television is informative and helpful to many people; Wildmon said such discussions often help legitimize what he considers immoral behavior. Donahue chided Wildmon for trying to censor TV; Wildmon said he has no power, only the opportunity to persuade and the right to try. Wildmon defended his threatened boycott of TV sponsors as both American and democratic. Donahue said advertisers were too scared to withstand such pressure.

And so it went, a fencing match between a clever city boy and clever country boy, with neither side puncturing a vital organ. The audience frequently voted for one man or the other by applause, boos and hisses. Support seemed evenly divided. It was a good show, and a high spirited one.

Both men came out looking good, through an on-camera appearance by Donahue's beautiful, charming wife, Marlon Thomas, was a bit much - especially when she talked about what a great guy her beleaguered husband is. Whether intended or not, it smacked of a stunt designed to win sympathy and support for Donahue.

People are forever surprised when Wildmon waltzes through the spotlight of public attention and emerges unscathed. Many people, such as the folks at CBS who dreamed up last June's disastrous

Wildmon-Mater debate, seem to think he is so hickish, so wrong, and so ignorant that mere exposure will cause him to dry up and blow away. Previously, the strategy was to ignore him. From time to time, there have been full-scale counterattacks. Nothing has worked.

What Wildmon's opponents fail to grasp is that he's surviving, thriving and gaining influence because he is a) sincere, b) smart and c) more than a little right.

I've had numerous discussions with Wildmon, and I've attacked and defended his various actions. Although I have many misgivings about some of his views, I have no doubt that he is fundamentally decent, a well-intentioned man who believes, correctly, that television is a major cultural force in our society. Given a choice between believing Wildmon and believing most of the many network executives I've met, I'd opt for Wildmon.

Wildmon sees TV as a great molder and shaper of values and beliefs. He thinks it is much too important to be left in the hands of greedy executives whose only motive is profit. And he thinks the tube has a wrongheaded value system.

You may not agree with Wildmon's moral code, but he has one, and he makes no apologies for it. He thinks sex is a beautiful gift from God that belongs in the marital bed. He objects to drinking and profanity. He cherishes family life, opposes homosexuality, and thinks people should worship God. He claims to love all people, from gays to murderers, but not necessarily their acts.

"We're all God's children," he's fond of saying. Wildmon is that rare breed of Christian fundamentalist who doesn't seem to have a mean streak.

When Wildmon looks at television, he sees a medium brimming with promiscuity, profanity, violence, alcoholic beverages and irreverence. Religious people are shown as fools, he asserts, family life is distorted, and traditional Christian values are woefully underrepresented. To those who prescribe the TV set's off button as a cure for such video ills, Wildmon says that's like fighting crime in the streets by staying inside. Now here's what's important about the assertions in this paragraph: Wildmon is right. And that's why he won't go away.

Wildmon has a faith in the masses that lets him believe that one man, speaking out from the obscurity of Tupelo, Mississippi, can make a difference. Like a minister with a calling, he is convinced that he must try. And he is trying, sometimes stubbing his toe along the way, but always trying. He says he doesn't want to control every show that goes out over the public airwaves, but he would like to have his values represented fully and fairly by them.

Wildmon has reasoned that commercial television responds only to commercial pressures; that you can't appeal to a network's morals, but you can appeal to its profits. Therefore, he applies his muscle to advertisers, urging them not to sponsor certain types of programming and threatening to boycott them if they don't comply. Wildmon notes, again correctly, that boycotts are part of the democratic process. Remember the civil rights boycotts of the last 1960s?

Too often, the response to this deceptively complex man has been a simpleminded attack rather than a thoughtful effort to understand and explain him. Wildmon is the leader of an important, perilous, and somewhat remarkable movement. There are reasons he and his movement exists. And neither will disappear until those reasons disappear.

SECTION FIVE • APPENDIX

What We Are Up Against

APPENDIX 1

Humanism, American's new national religion

This section is adapted from *Christianity and Humanism*, a study written by Steve Hallman in 1984 while he was a vice president of National Federation for Decency (AFA).

⁂

America has a new national religion. Well, it isn't exactly new but it is national. Most Americans have never heard of it, but a high percentage of them would agree with much of what humanists believe.

This religion is the religion of choice for thousands of influential members in the media, law, politics, education and other avenues of influence. Ask any of these people if they are a humanist and they will ask you to explain what you are asking about. You see, they are humanists, but they don't know they are humanists.

Just what is humanism? It is a godless religion that has made rapid gains in our society in the past few years. Some would argue there are more humanists in America than evangelicals.

In our research, we studied only Humanist Manifesto I and II. These two documents clearly define the humanist beliefs. Humanist III and IV are available for those who desire to go deeper. Much more information on humanism can be found by searching the Internet. You can find info on the American Humanist Association at AmericanHumanist.org.

Background and Growth of Humanism

The story goes that Rip Van Winkle fell asleep in the Catskill Mountains one day. When he awoke twenty years later, he discovered he had slept through a revolution. Many say the Church is sleeping through a revolution of a different sort: a revolution not fought with guns and swords, but with ideas and philosophies. And what is at stake in this conflict is the very foundation of Western civilization.

The conflict is one of values, and which values will be the standard for our society and the base for our system of justice. For over 200 years our country has based its morals, its sense of right and wrong, on the Christian view of man. The Ten Commandments and the Sermon on the Mount have been our solid foundation. To be sure, we have never managed to get the system perfect in practice. But it has been the most nearly perfect system ever devised in the history of mankind.

Today there are those who would have us change, go in new directions, directions they are convinced will free man from his chains of oppression. They call their belief system "humanism," a term which refers to a world view starting with humans, not God.

They strive for a new secular society in which moral standards will come from within themselves. One of their stated goals is to achieve as soon as possible a secular and humanist world community.

As humanism becomes firmly entrenched in a culture, two things happen to the church. First, the church loses its ability to influence society. And, second, the church loses its respect in society. Our need to carefully examine the movement is painfully obvious.

For years, Christians have been vaguely aware that an anti-Christian sentiment was operating in society. It was really nothing new. We knew certain forces were at work to undermine the church, but we blamed it on the devil and left it at that.

But we only touched part of the problem. We said, "Something's wrong. The church has lost its power." But our charges lacked specificity.

This study is designed to be specific. It is an attempt to define terminology, examine basic tenets of humanism, and contrast the movement with Christianity.

The church, the body of Christ, must begin to understand the nature of humanism, a system which has no place for a supernatural God or a Savior who died for sinners.

The aims of this study are to answer three basic questions:
1. What is humanism?
2. What is the impact of humanism?
3. What is the Christian response?

These aims are developed in six chapters touching on key aspects of the movement which directly or indirectly affect the Church.

Humanism is not related to those who study the humanities

What is humanism? When we use the term "humanism" we are not talking about humanitarianism--being sensitive and kind to other humans. All Christians should be humanitarian. It was said of Jesus He went about doing good.

In the narrowest sense, a humanist is a person interested in the humanities: the study of literature, history, fine arts and the classics. But today, the self-definition of "humanism" as advanced by the American Humanist Association and other humanist organizations means a way of life and a set of beliefs which begins with man, not God. It is the religion which holds that man is the measure of all things and the center of all things. For humanists, belief in God is something illusory and destructive.

In this study, the adjective "secular" will sometimes be applied to avoid confusion. The term derives from the Latin *saeculum*, which means "time" or "age." To call someone secular means he is completely time-bound, a person whose hope is confined to the here and now. A secular humanist is a creature of this world who sees belief in anything "other-worldly" as either meaningless or irrelevant to the human experience.

No room exists for a God who plays a vital role in human affairs.

In his book, **What is Secular Humanism?** Dr. James Hitchcock states, "Groups like the American Humanist Association are not humanists just in the sense they have an interest in the humanities or they value man over nature. In their self-definition, God does not exist.

"They promote a way of life that systematically excludes God and all religion in the traditional sense. Man, for better or worse, is on his own in the universe. He marks the highest point to which nature has yet evolved and he must rely entirely on his own resources."

What are the basic tenets of humanism? What do humanists believe? Basic tenets of the faith are formulated and recorded in two documents, Humanist Manifesto I and Humanist Manifesto II.

Humanist Manifesto I was published in 1973, and hailed as a "philosophy of survival" by the New York Times. Humanist Manifesto II included the following signers: Betty Friedan, founder of the National Organization of Women; influential philosophers Brand Blanshard, Antony Flew, Sidney Hook, John Herman Randall, Jr., and Sir Alfred Ayer; Isaac Asimov, author; prominent scientists Fancis Crick, Andrei Sakharov, Zhores Medvedev, and Herbert Muller; B.F. Skinner, Professor of Psychology, Harvard; Corliss Lamont, Chairman, National Emergency Civil Liberties Commission; Joseph Fletcher, professor, author, a leading proponent of 'situation ethics' in the United States"; Allen F. Guttmacher, President, Planned Parenthood Federation of America; Lawrence Lader, Chairman of the National Association for the Repeal of Abortion Laws; Paul Kurtz, Editor, The Humanist; Gunnar Myrdal, Swedish economist with worldwide influence.

Key leaders have more influence

The list of signers of Humanist Manifesto II was considerably longer than the first, indicating humanism had gained respect in the intervening forty years. And there are more signers today. Many of the signers of the various Humanist Manifestos are today strategically placed in highly influential areas of public life. They have the power to influence public opinion far in excess of their numerical strength.

Humanist Manifesto I and Humanist Manifesto II are somewhat the old and new testaments of humanism. Each of the following statements is taken verbatim from these two documents:

"Religious humanists regard the universe as self-existing and not created…Humanism believes that man is a part of nature and that he has emerged as the result of a continuous process. Humanists are firmly convinced that existing acquisitive and profit motivated society has shown itself to be inadequate and that a radical change in methods, controls and motives must be instituted.

"Humanists believe that traditional theism, especially faith in the prayer-hearing God, assumed to love and care for persons, to hear and understand their prayers, and to be able to do something about them, is an unproved and outmoded faith. Salvationism based on mere affirmation, still appears as harmful, diverting people with false hopes of heaven hereafter. Reasonable minds must look to other means for survival.

"We find insufficient evidence for belief in the existence of a supernatural; it is either meaningless or irrelevant to the question of the survival and fulfillment of the human race…no deity will save us; we must save ourselves.

"Ethics is autonomous and situational, needing no theological or ideological sanction.

"Reason and intelligence are the most effective instruments that humankind possesses. There is no substitute; neither faith nor passion…

"In the area of sexuality, we believe that intolerant attitudes, often cultivated by orthodox religions and puritanical cultures, unduly repress sexual conduct. While we do not approve of exploitive, denigrating forms of sexual expression, neither do we wish to prohibit, by law or social sanction, sexual behavior between consenting adults. The many varieties of sexual exploration should not in themselves be considered evil.

"The right to … abortion … should be recognized. To enhance

freedom and dignity the individual must experience a full range of civil liberties in all societies. This includes…recognition of an individual's right to die with dignity, euthanasia, and the right to suicide.

"The separation of church and state and the separation of ideology and state are imperatives. The state should encourage maximum freedom for different moral, political, religious, and social values in society. It should not favor any particular religious bodies through the use of public monies, nor espouse a single ideology and function thereby as an instrument of propaganda or oppression, particularly against dissenters … People are more important than decalogues, rules, proscriptions, or regulations. We look to the development of a system of world law and a world order based on transnational federal government."

Humanism is an old religion

What is the background of humanism? The framework for humanism was provided by the Sophists, about 500 B.C. It was Protagoras the Sophist, who said, "Man is the measure of all things." Sophists were humanists who attempted to replace the age of theology with that of rationalism.

The second wave of humanism came in the 14th century with the movement called the Renaissance, or the "rebirth of learning." Renaissance humanists revived the study of "humane" as opposed to sacred literature. What began as a seemingly good and harmless interest in the classics developed into a completely secular system, rejecting God and exalting man. It was a system of thought which made man the center of values. Man was the total authority and there were no absolutes.

These later humanists saw man as a creature of the world; not a creature of God. The religion of culture began to replace Christian religion. "Culture became the faith of the 15th and 16th century humanists."

Humanism enjoyed its most rapid growth in the twentieth century. Three dates are extremely significant.

In 1933, a group of thirty-four liberal humanists in the United

States agreed on some basic principles of humanism and established their religious beliefs in the document Human Manifesto I.

You might call it an affirmation of faith for the humanist. This first creed used the word "religion" to describe the movement, but strongly rejected the connection of their religion with any deity other than man.

One of the first statements in Humanist Manifesto I reads, "There is great danger of a final, and we believe fatal, identification of the word "religion" with doctrines and methods which have lost their significance and which are powerless to solve the problems of humans living in the twentieth century."

The main author of Humanist Manifesto I was John Dewey, probably the most influential American philosopher, especially in the field of public education.

In 1961 the U.S. Supreme Court cited secular humanism as a religion in the case of *Torcaso v. Watkins*. Roy Torcaso, a humanist living in Maryland had refused to declare his belief in Almighty God, which was required by state law in order for him to be commissioned as a notary public. The Court ruled that requirement for such an oath "invades appellant's freedom of belief and religion."

Footnote 11 of the *Torcaso v. Watkins* decision contains the Court's citation of secular humanism as a religion: "Among religions in this country which do not teach what would generally be considered a belief in God are Buddhism, Taoism, Ethical Culture, secular humanism, and others."

In 1973 influential humanists, many of them well known in our society, got together to update the religious creed of Humanist Manifesto I. Humanist Manifesto II appeared. Its authors called it "an expression of a living and growing faith."

Humanism is a dangerous religion

What danger does the humanist movement pose for the church? Humanists believe faith in God is harmful to the individual and dangerous to society. Therefore, all influence of Christian faith must be removed from society. To achieve this end, humanists feel obligated and duty-bound to use whatever methods are available.

This necessitates the establishing of humanism as the rule for law and justice in our society, the establishing of a system of law under-girded and guided by humanist thought. According to George Gallup, the overwhelming people of this country identify with the Christian faith. Realizing this, humanists have lobbied hard for laws to remove Christianity from meaningful participation in government, law and the public school classroom – in effect, establishing humanism as the defacto state religion.

Christians must not lose sight of the fact that the laws of every society are based upon some philosophy regarded by individuals responsible for the laws as being the highest good achievable for society. And, while not all the founding fathers of the United States were Christian, they did generally share the Christian view of morality and participated in establishing that view into law.

Professor Harvey Cox, in his book *The Secular City*, writes, "Secular humanism is a dangerous ideological system because it seeks to impose its ideology through the organs of the State. Because secular humanism has no tolerance and is opposed to other religions, it actively rejects, excludes and attempts to eliminate traditional theism from meaningful participation in the American culture."

Part of the problem has been the failure of Christians to observe the feverish activity among humanists to bring about their goal of a totally secular society in America. Christians have seen the symptoms, but failed to recognize the disease.

Humanists understand humanism and Christianity are incompat-ible. In fact humanists view Christians as natural enemies. But because of defective thinking, many Christians have failed to see the danger of the movement, and assumed humanists are willing for the two to exist in harmony. We have much to learn.

Humanism, simply stated, is the religion which denies God and deifies man – the religion which makes human consciousness the alpha and omega of all things. Secular humanism and Christianity operate on two totally different world views. One says "man is lord." The other says "Jesus is Lord."

Here is where humanists get their ethics

Humanist Manifesto II: "We affirm that moral values derive their source from human experience. Ethics is autonomous and situational, needing no theological or ideological sanction. Ethics stems from human need and interest. We strive for the good life, here and now."

What is the basis for humanist ethics? "Ethics is autonomous…" The word "autonomous" comes from the Greek autos, self, and nomos, law. Disciples of this thinking are literally a law unto themselves. It follows there are no laws or rights given by God. Ethics are based on what seems necessary or expedient at the time. Man is his own and only authority.

"Ethics is…situational." The true humanist believes in a system of personal morality and ethics often termed situation ethics. Situation ethics is morality and personal ethics based on the premise there are no absolutes. Right and wrong cannot be determined by a set of rules and certainly not by commandments given by God. It follows that moral values are a product of human choice. Each individual must choose what is right for himself without regard to any set of pre-existing standards. Ethics and morals are based on the current situation and how one feels about the situation. No standard exists to judge any act as right or wrong.

Humanists and Christians have different source for morality

Jacques Monod, the French biologist, who subscribed to the humanist world view, said in his book *Chance and Necessity*, there is no way to determine the "ought" from the "is." So what is approved or disapproved is determined by "human need and interest." Therefore there can be no fixed point of reference to judge the rightness or wrongness of any activity. Secular humanists reject the Biblical imperatives which declare certain absolutes such as, "You shall not murder.... You shall not commit adultery.... You shall not steal.... You shall not give false witness against your neighbor...." (Genesis 20:13-16 KJV).

Where can we see humanist ethics at work in society? There are varying degrees of commitment to the stated creed found in Humanist Manifestoes I and II, just as there are varying degrees of commitment to the value system of Christianity. For instance, one can be deeply ingrained in the humanist affirmation of situation ethics without denying the existence of God. For example, some humanists might say, "It is okay to believe in God as long as it doesn't affect the way you act or live." This milder form of humanism is growing rapidly in our society.

The rapid spread of humanist ethics owes much to the positive, sympathetic treatment by the entertainment media. We must add the rise of other media – such as music, movies, videos, internet and a host of the social media instruments – have supported television's attack on Christian values in recent years. Television has shaped and molded many of our ideas. And since television appeals mainly to the emotional rather than the rational, it can be a tremendous instrument of change. Humanists have found television makes a wonderful pulpit for the preaching of humanist ethics.

TV pushes humanist morals

A case in point was a CBS made-for-TV movie called **Not In Front Of The Children**. The movie centered on a mother who chose to live with a man without benefit of marriage. Her ex-husband is represented as a Christian.

The drama opens with tender, heart-warming music surrounding scenes of affection between mother, children and mother's live-in boyfriend. Music stops. It is Sunday morning. Enter one obviously narrow-minded father who is upset at the thought of his children living under the same roof with mother and boyfriend.

Husband: "Nancy, you are the person they (daughters) respect most in the whole world, and you're teaching them that intimacy outside marriage is not a sin."

Wife: "I don't think it is. ... I am being honest with them. ... I am doing what's right for me, and later on they can do what's right for them."

Husband: "If you deliberately choose to have a relationship with some man, that's your right and your choice, even if I don't approve. But what about their rights? They didn't choose to live with this man."

Wife: "I asked them. They wanted to."

Husband: "They're babies! They don't know what it means. I forbid you to flaunt this relationship in front of my children." (Husband leaves.)

Daughter (who has overheard conversation): "Mom, are you gonna go to hell?"

Mother: "No, sweetheart, I'm not. This is kind of hard to explain. ... Everyone has their own beliefs. And your Daddy thinks the way we're living together is wrong. He has a right to think that. But I don't. I believe God is love, and that what we have together, Paul (her live-in companion) and I (beautiful, moving inspirational music starts again) and you two girls, that's love. And I think God understands that. That's what I believe. And, when you two girls are all grown up, then you have a right to decide what's right for you. OK?"

Daughter: "OK. I knew God wouldn't send you to hell." (Music intensifies)."

The remainder of the program is a study in contrasts. At one end of the spectrum is the harsh, bigoted, dogmatic, intolerant, domineering, ill-tempered, biased and overbearing Christian ex-husband. At the other end are the sympathetic, caring, kind, affectionate, gentle, understanding, tender, benevolent, secular living-together lovers. Throughout the program, the injured party is the teary-eyed ex-wife who is consistently a victim of Christian intolerance.

This and countless other entertainment media productions in recent years have been quite effective in encouraging the "what's right for me" value system as opposed to the Christian value system.

The program above illustrates well the humanist view of ethics. Sex outside marriage is right because it is decided by the parties involved that it serves their needs and interests. Later on in life the girls would decide what is "right for them" on the basis of their needs and interests. In the humanist ethics system, personal values are relative, needing no other sanction than that expressed by the mother above, "I'm doing what's right for me."

Public education is one place where humanism is promoted

How are the moral values of humanist ethics formed? Since "moral values derive their source from human experience" and personal ethics need no "theological or ideological sanction," it follows the past has no precedents for the future. Parental values are not necessarily important for children, and values based on religion are not acceptable. Personal values must come from within.

One arena in which humanists have been able to advance their system of ethics is the field of public education. "Values Clarification" courses being taught in many schools today advocate the development of personal values which are purely "situational and autonomous." The values clarification approach was formulated by Louis Raths who borrowed heavily from the thinking of John Dewey. Raths was concerned not with the content of people's values, but the process of valuing.

In the values clarification system, to arrive at a child's values, the child should:

1. Choose the value freely. He is to choose the value free from parental guidance and religious teachings. In the book, **Values Clarification**, *A Handbook of Practical Strategies for Teachers and Students*, edited by Sidney Simon and others, the statement is made "young people brought up by moralizing adults are not prepared to make their own responsible choices." And the problem with depending on religious teachings, according to the same authors, is that "we have religious people who love

their neighbors on the Sabbath and spend the rest of the week competing with them."

2. Choose from alternatives. The child is to choose from alternatives including those different from those of his or her parents: alternatives such as to have premarital sex or not to have premarital sex.

3. Choose after considering the consequences. This assumes a child is able to see far enough ahead to be the best judge of those consequences.

4. Prize and cherish the value, publicly affirming when appropriate. If one cannot point to a value with pride then it must be called into question. This includes religious values.

5. Act on the value regularly and consistently. This is supposed to help students see when their stated values and their actions are out of harmony. The process is supposed to help students discover what they really value. If a student says he or she values church but seldom attends, the values clarification approach may cause the student to decide church is not as important as was supposed.

One popular values clarification technique is called "values voting." In this system, the teacher begins with the question, "How many of you here …" and students are asked to respond before all other students in the affirmative, the negative, or with no vote at all. Questions suggested in the values clarification handbook previously mentioned include: "How many of you here … approve of premarital sex for boys? …approve of premarital sex for girls? … would approve of a marriage between homosexuals being sanctioned by priest, minister or rabbi? … would encourage legal abortion for an unwed daughter? … have spoken with homosexuals about their lifestyles? … would take your children to religious services even if they didn't want to go? … would be upset if organized religion disappeared?"

Here is how Christians should respond

In short, the values clarification approach is a model for developing situation ethics in children and youth. The student must question his present value system and somehow develop a new one which has not been "imposed" by his parents or the church.

What is the Christian response to humanist ethics? Humanist ethics reduced to its simplest form means situations, not rules, determine ethics. What is the Christian response? Certainly we need to examine the system of humanist ethics. But more importantly, we need to get a firm grip on the principles of Christian ethics.

Humanist ethics says values are relative and subjective, and individuals may follow their autonomous opinions without regard to moral truth. Morality in this system can be reduced to efficiency in attaining specific objectives. The basis for Christian ethics stands in bold contrast.

Christian ethics is based on the Word of God and the revelation of God in Jesus Christ. Christians are called to do what Jesus did, to have the ethics of Jesus as revealed in the New Testament. Turning from sin, Christians make a decision for Christ, accept by faith the terms of the Covenant sealed with His blood, believe in God's faithfulness to His promises, and live by the love which is the gift of the Holy Spirit. Faithfully following of the truth as revealed in the Bible has always been the strength of Christian ethics.

The Bible has something to say about every area of life. There are Biblical absolutes that do not vary according to circumstances or situations. To be sure, these absolute norms have never been applied perfectly because imperfect people have never been able to carry them out perfectly. However, when Biblical principles have been applied to lives and consequently to society, both individuals and society have benefited. To be sure, humanism, advancing its causes from many strategic pressure points in society, has affected Christianity and the Church.

Perhaps the humanist claim of no absolutes, no judgment, no need for theological sanction, and consequently a system in which one must be careful to judge no particular action as sinful – perhaps that thinking has diluted the theology and the message of the Church. Could it be this is the philosophy which has led to the popular maxim, "It doesn't matter what you believe, as long as you're sincere?"

Yet Biblical absolutes of right and wrong remain. The Ten Commandments and the spirit of their application as given in the Sermon on the Mount remains our strong base for personal morality and ethics.

In summary, Christian ethics are based on specific, revealed moral truths contained in the Bible. These truths are absolute and unalterable. But Christian ethics are not limited to specific laws and truths. The life of Jesus and the Sermon on the Mount are filled with directives for daily living.

A guiding principle for developing Christian ethics is the basic affirmation "Jesus is Lord." Each Christian must learn the dynamics of putting Jesus at the center of life and subjecting everything else to His Lordship. When actions and decisions are made on the principle of the Lordship of Christ, one can properly be said to have Christian ethics.

The doctrine of man

Humanist Manifesto II: "We believe.... that traditional dogmatic or authoritarian religions that place revelation, God, ritual, or creed above human needs and experience do a disservice to the human species.... We find insufficient evidence for belief in the existence of a supernatural.... We begin with humans not God, nature not deity.... Humans are responsible for all that we are or will become. No deity will save us. We must save ourselves....

"Science affirms that the human species is an emergence from natural evolutionary forces. As far as we know, the total personality is a function of the biological organism transacting in a social and cultural context."

Humanism sees man alone in the universe. The true humanist is either agnostic (one who believes it is impossible to know whether there is a God) or atheistic (one who does not believe in God). He believes man is an accident of nature. Man is alone in the universe. He is his own god, responsible for his own salvation which is limited to the here and now. All that we are or ever hope to be is dependent on social and cultural experiences.

Isaac Asimov, a signer of Humanist Manifesto II, is one of the most prolific authors and science writers of all time. Also, his writings frequently appeared in the pornographic magazine *Playboy*. He is at least bluntly honest on this point: "Emotionally, I am an atheist. I don't have the evidence to prove God doesn't exist, but I so strongly suspect He doesn't that I don't waste my time."

Humanists reject both the idea of a transcendent God, and the revelation of God found in the Bible. For them, belief in God is something illusory, destructive and dangerous to the welfare of society. Humanists are pledged to the removal of all vestiges of the Bible and Christian teaching from society.

An article appearing in *The Humanist*, official publication of the American Humanist Association, states well the humanist position on the matter. The article, titled "A New Religion for a New Age," is written by John Dunphy.

Mr. Dunphy writes: "The Bible is not merely another book, an outmoded and archaic book, or even an extremely influential book; it has been and remains an incredibly dangerous book. It and the various Christian churches which are parasitic upon it have been directly responsible for most of the wars, persecutions, and outrages which humankind has perpetrated upon itself over the past two thousand years." He continues: "I am convinced the battle for humankind's future must be waged and won in the public classroom by teachers who correctly perceive their role as the proselytizers of a new faith.... These teachers must embody the same dedication as the most rabid fundamentalist preachers, for they will be ministers of another sort, utilizing a classroom instead of a pulpit to convey humanist values in whatever subject they teach.... The classroom must and will become an area of conflict between the old and the new: the rotting corpse of Christianity, together with all its adjacent evils and misery, and the new faith of humanism, resplendent in its promise of a world in which the never realized Christian ideal of 'love thy neighbor,' will finally be achieved."

Humanism, evolution are brothers

Humanism embraces naturalistic evolution. Humanism affirms man evolved through a process of naturalistic evolution. This is an integral part of their religious doctrines. The humanist creed leaves no place for a transcendent Creator God.

In their search for the origins of man, humanists go back to the evolutionary theory of Charles Darwin. The theory holds man came into being as a result of forces operating in nature independent of any supernatural deity. Man is an accidental species. Although Darwin never fully abandoned the conviction there is a God, many of his followers have done so. By making man the product of "natural selection," Darwin's humanist followers have devised a doctrine of man which releases man from any responsibility to his Creator and any obligation to heed the Creator's laws. Darwinism, by removing the origin of man from God's direct activity, undermines any view of a divine order to nature.

The humanist idea of man as a creature of evolution has become basic to the thinking of many in strategic positions in society. A good illustration of this thinking is found in the words of an article issued in *Pediatrics* (journal of American Pediatrics Association) which reads: "We can no longer base our ethics on the idea that human beings are a special form of creation, made in the image of God, singled out from all the other animals, and alone possessing an immortal soul."

Right at this point, Christians have given much ground which quite possibly may never be regained. Naturalistic evolution has been a part of higher education for a long time now. How easily intimidated we become these days when questions are raised which seem to deny the Biblical account of creation. But let us not forget one important fact. From the very beginning, the vast majority of people in this country have believed "God created." So the burden of proof lies not with Christians. God's revealed word has withstood critics for centuries.

Can evolution make a Boeing 747?

The burden of proof lies with those who say man came into being another way, with those who believe an unknown life form arose by some unknown process in an unknown ocean of unknown chemicals, in contact with unknown particles bombarded with unknown energies from an unknown source. Sir Fred Hoyle, the distinguished British astronomer, likened the prospects of higher life forms emerging by evolution as comparable with the chances a tornado sweeping through a junk-yard might assemble a Boeing 747 from the materials therein.

And yet naturalistic evolution can be taught as scientific fact in the public classroom. In this arena, humanism has experienced phenomenal success.

Why this hard line on evolution? If the humanist admits to a "creative spark," then he also must admit to a Creator God. The only alternative to naturalistic evolution is creation. No matter how improbable for the true humanist, life must have originated from chance. The idea of a transcendent Creator God is unthinkable.

It is this kind of irrationality that pervades the humanist view of the origin of man. There just simply is no place for God. Long ago the Psalmist gave this evaluation: "The fool hath said in his heart, 'There is no God.'" (Ps. 14:1) The Bible boldly declares, "In the beginning God" (Genesis 1:1 KJV) In the Scriptures God doesn't spend much time trying to prove His own existence. The beauty and majesty of His creation give witness to His being. In answer to the question, Who made all things? The Scripture declares, "God created." (Genesis 1:1) The Biblical message is God is Creator, and nature is His handiwork.

In Genesis 1:1-2:3, we see an all-powerful Creator-God who simply speaks and order springs into being, providing a rich, well-balanced, beautiful dwelling place for his highest creation of all, man. "Then God said, 'Let us make man in our image, in our likeness.'" (Genesis

1:26) Man was the crowning work of God's creative acts. He was not a miniature replica of God, but was created to be the bearer of spiritual distinctions marking him as uniquely related to God and as higher than the animals. These things are true not because we can subject them to the scientific method and prove them to be true. They are true because God has revealed them as truth in His Word.

Evolution can be taught, but intelligent design cannot

If this basic of all affirmations is questioned, again the burden of proof lies with the humanist, not with the Christian. Humanism targets children. It is remarkable that although the theory of evolution cannot be proven by empirical scientific data, it has become almost universally accepted in our universities. Science and biology books in public classrooms contain the theory of evolution to be taught as though it were fact. Like evolution, Biblical creationism cannot be proven by empirical scientific data.

Yet, it has been banned from public school curricula. This is in spite of the fact many scientists now accept the Genesis account of Creation. It was Dr. Werner von Braun who said, "Anything as well ordered and perfectly created as is our earth and universe must have a Maker, a master Designer. Anything so orderly, so perfect, so precisely balanced, so majestic as this creation can only be the product of a Divine Idea. There must be a Maker; there can be no other way."

Humanists have for years weaved naturalistic evolution into the fabric of popular children's books. Most children are familiar with the Berenstain Bears. Jan and Stan Berenstain have written many books which are loved by very young children. In one book, Papa Bear explains to his son, "Nature is you, nature is me. It's all that is or was or ever will be." Berenstain is saying the same thing to our children as Carl Sagan said to millions when he opened his series **Cosmos**, on PBS, with the statement, "The cosmos is all that is or ever was or ever will be." This is basic to the belief of the humanist faith.

Another children's book, written by humanist Chris Brockman, is called *What About Gods?* One of the sections illustrates well the humanist faith in man as totally independent of God. Brockman says to the children, "We no longer need gods to explain how things happen. By carefully thinking, measuring, testing we have discovered many of the real causes of things, and we're discovering more all the time. We call this thinking."

Humanism sees no inherent sanctity in human life. With the humanist view man is an accidental animal, and life is a product of natural forces. It follows there are no higher laws governing the sanctity, worth and dignity of human life than those man constructs for himself. Therefore, in the absence of any Creator or Lawgiver, the humanist boldly declares belief in the human right to suicide, abortion and euthanasia. And one follows another. Suicide is the act of self-destruction. Abortion is the destruction of unwanted, inconvenient, unborn human life. Euthanasia is the destruction of the life of the helpless, hopeless, children or adults. This act is often referred to as "mercy killing."

If one believes man is merely a "biological organism," and "no deity will save us, we must save ourselves," then we very easily get into a system of trade-offs in order to "save ourselves." To make things more comfortable for the post-birth population, humanism affirms a system which sanctions the killing of unwanted individuals, a system which in America at present is denying life to one and a half million unborn babies each year.

Already in this country, we have infanticide quietly practiced by doctors who, acting on the wishes of the parents, allow children born with birth defects to starve to death. The measure is called "non-treatment." One case, which got national coverage, involved a baby in Indiana who had Down's syndrome, and needed serious but feasible surgery for an intestinal disorder. The parents recommended "non-treatment" and the child was starved to death. It took six days for the infant to die. His life was imperfect and expendable.

With the skyrocketing cost of health care in America and the growing number of elderly, one wonders if they could ultimately be caught in the trade-offs. If no God exists to declare human life sacred, and if "we must save ourselves," who knows what arbitrary values will govern human life in the future?

In summary, humanism views man as a creature of nature, coming from nowhere, going nowhere, whose life is limited to the here and now. It is a religion, which has no place for God and certainly no place for a Man who through His suffering and death on a cross calls men to repentance. Belief in Jesus Christ is said to be harmful to the welfare of society.

The Christian, however, cannot, must not accept this materialistic view of man. While the Christian fully recognizes the need for the material, he also knows man cannot live by bread alone. He has a Creator and without a loving relationship with his Creator, life will always be incomplete no matter how much harmony he finds with his environment.

Human Sexuality

Humanist Manifesto II: "In the area of sexuality, we believe that intolerant attitudes, often cultivated by orthodox religions and puritanical cultures, unduly repress sexual conduct…. While we do not approve of exploitive, denigrating forms of sexual expression, neither do we wish to prohibit, by law or social sanction, sexual behavior between consenting adults. The many varieties of sexual exploration should not in themselves be considered evil."

Humanists believe Christianity represses sexual conduct. Humanism as expressed in Humanist Manifestoes I and II blames Christianity and other religions for intolerant, repressive attitudes concerning sex. Humanism teaches Christians are responsible for attitudes leading to the thinking that sex is bad and sex is sinful. Humanists blame a variety of sexual dysfunctions on puritanical upbringing and defective teaching on sex by Christian parents and Christian ministers. Christians have made sex to be something negative and demeaning according to the humanist view.

Humanists believe all varieties of sexual expression are acceptable as long as no one forces another. No type of sexual behavior between consenting adults should be prohibited. Sexual promiscuity can be a healthy and normal response to one's needs and interests. Sexual behavior is said to be a private matter and none of society's business.

Anything goes

Humanists believe any sex act agreeable to consenting parties is acceptable. Therefore no standard exists to judge the rightness or wrongness of homosexuality, incest or any other deviant sexual behavior. These beliefs oppose Biblical imperatives which place sex within the confines of a loving relationship between husband and wife. In Proverbs the fifth chapter, young men are instructed to abstain from adultery. Then the young man is told how to fulfill his sexual needs, in sexual union with his wife. To do so will fill him with happiness and will bless his life. (Proverbs 5:18,19 KJV)

Humanists consider varieties of sexual expression of value. There are no sexual taboos. Any sexual act is to be judged according to whether it fulfills the needs and interests of the persons performing the act. The only restriction according to Humanist Manifesto II is humans are not to be treated as sex objects.

Humanists believe man, being a product of naturalistic evolution, must form his own standards of acceptable and non-acceptable sexual behavior. The term "evil" is to be rejected when referring to any of the varieties of sexual expression.

Scripture, on the other hand, is clear that although sex is a God-given human drive, it also can be used wrongly. When used wrongly it becomes destructive and constitutes sin.

The teachings of humanism and Christianity stand in bold contrast at this point. Basic to Christian beliefs is knowing and applying what

God teaches about human sexuality leads to wholeness in that area, that human sexuality has some God-given boundaries, and there are absolutes involved. The Biblical perspective is adultery is wrong. It violates one of the Ten Commandments. Whereas adultery is glorified and accepted in the secular humanist philosophy, Scripture paints a different picture.

Entertainment pushes humanistic view of sex

Solomon stated it this way: "My son, pay attention to my wisdom, listen to my words of insight, that you may maintain discretion and your lips may preserve knowledge. For the lips of an adulteress drip honey. And her speech is smoother than oil; but in the end she is bitter as gall, sharp as a double-edged sword. Her feet go down to death; her steps lead straight to the grave. She gives no thought to the way of life; her paths are crooked, but she knows it not. Now then my sons, listen to me; do not turn aside from what I say. Keep a path far from her, do not go near the door of her house." (Proverbs 5:1-8 KJV)

Humanist attitudes toward sex are promoted through the entertainment media. Humanists have found the entertainment media to be a very effective means for the promotion of humanist teaching on sex. Take, for instance, an NBC network presentation of **Different Strokes**, normally considered a "family series." The series was begun as the heartwarming story of a wealthy businessman who adopted two poor black children.

Mr. Drummond, or Dad in the series, had generally been portrayed as having high standards and traditional values. But in one particular episode he suddenly stepped out of character and lied to the children to cover up his own immorality.

A weekend camping trip was set up for the children. A friend, Miss Saunders, persuaded Mr. Drummond to opt for a couple of days, and nights, with her. So Dad cancelled his plans with the children and sent the housekeeper on the camping trip. The children came home only to find Dad sleeping with Miss Saunders.

Arnold, the youngest of the children couldn't understand what was happening. So Dad explained his involvement with the woman to young Arnold. He explained he was a man and Miss Sunders was a woman, and what he did was normal grown-up behavior.

In effect, he said sexual involvement and marriage should not necessarily be related.

Later, when Miss Saunders attempted a quick exit, the family insisted she stay the remainder of the weekend.

The program ended with Little Arnold proudly expressing his sexual enlightenment. He said, "We understand, we're all adults here."

The clear and unmistakable teaching was sex outside marriage is normal and acceptable.

Humanists will continue to censor Christians

Humanism totally rejects the Christian perspective that sex is a wonderful gift from God, and sex inside marriage is wonderfully fulfilling, wonderfully right, and sex outside marriage is wrong. Scripture says God created Adam and Eve and blessed the sexual relationship between husband and wife as he said to them: "Be fruitful and multiply and increase in number; fill the earth and subdue it." (Genesis 1:27, 28 KJV)

As long as television is dominated by humanist interests, traditional values on human sexuality will continue to take a beating. Why? Because ninety-eight percent of homes in America have televisions. There are more TV's in America than bathtubs. The average television stays on more than seven hours a day. By the time a person has finished high school, the average child has spent some 15,000 hours in front of the TV, actually more time than in school. So television is a tremendously powerful value transmitter. It has transmitted some decidedly secular humanist ideas on sexuality in recent years. That is not a judgment. It is based on sound research.

The humanistic value orientation of TV writers and producers came through loud and clear in a study by Stanley Rothman, Linda Lichter and Robert Lichter published in *Public Opinion Magazine*. The survey involved 104 producers, writers and TV executives, people who are directly responsible for what we see on television. While the study was done some years ago, the stats, no doubt, would be approximately the same.

Of these people, 25 percent say they were raised in some Protestant denomination, 12 percent as Catholics and 59 percent in the Jewish faith. However, 93 percent say they now seldom or never attend church. Four out of five do not regard homosexual relations as wrong. Eighty-six percent support the right of professing homosexuals to teach in public schools. Only 17 percent strongly agree adultery is wrong. Ninety-seven percent believe a woman has the right to decide for herself whether to have an abortion.

Furthermore, members of this group believe it is okay to use television to reshape society to fit their desired mold. To quote the researchers: "Two out of three believe TV entertainment should be a major force for social reform." And what kind of social reform do they favor? From the study cited above, coupled with what is obvious as one views modern primetime television, one can only conclude it is secular humanist reform that the media elite actively seek. In the same study, media members were asked to rank social groups in the order of influence the groups should have in society. Only the military ranked lower than religion in the order of influence which the TV elite want groups to have in their new social structure.

Commenting on this same trend, James Hitchcock, Professor of History at the University of St. Louis said, "It is the mass media which, more than anything else accounts for the rapid spread of secularism in the late twentieth century."

We all know a sexual revolution took place in America during the sixties and seventies, and continued on into the eighties. It was a secular humanist sexual revolution. According to Dr. Hitchcock, the revolution was achieved in a number of ways. "On the simplest level, it consisted of talking about what was hitherto unmentionable. Subjects previously forbidden in the popular media (e.g. abortion, incest) were presented for the first time. In the beginning these presentations were brief, cautious, and blandly neutral. There were cries of protest. These were met with boasts about how "tastefully" the subjects had been dealt with. "After all," the argument ran, "knowledge is better than ignorance."

What many failed to realize was the unsuitability of the mass media to address such issues in the first place. Television networks are in competition with each other to attract the largest possible audience. By its very nature, television deals with such problems briefly, simplistically and sensationally, hoping to grab viewers away from the other networks.

Hitchcock echoes the sentiments of many concerned Christians when he says, "No matter how seemingly 'neutral' the treatment, when certain ideas are given time and space in the media they acquire a respectability that increases with frequency. Then comes the point where previously taboo subjects become familiar and acceptable. There is deep hypocrisy in the media's pious claims they merely reflect reality and do not shape it. In fact, the power of celebrity is used deliberately and selectively in order to effect change in values."

Humanist view of sex vs. Christian view

Christians must affirm sex as a God-given gift to be enjoyed in the bonds of marriage. We must live out the beauty and joy of a loving relationship as depicted in Proverbs 5:18: "May your fountain be blessed, and may you rejoice in the wife of your youth. A loving doe, a graceful deer... may you ever be captivated by her love."

We must dispel through correct teaching the notion that sex for the Christian is something bland and repressive. It should be just the opposite. Dr. Ed Wheat, in his book **Intended for Pleasure** describes well the New Testament perspective on sex in marriage: "As a matter of fact, the sex relationship in marriage receives such emphasis in the Scriptures we begin to see it was meant not only to be a wonderful, continuing experience for the husband and wife, but it also was intended to show us something wonderful about God and His relationship with us. Ephesians 5:31, 32 spells it out: "For this cause shall a man leave his father and mother, and shall be joined unto his wife, and the two shall be one flesh. This is a great mystery, but I speak concerning Christ and the church."

Thus, the properly and lovingly executed and mutually satisfying sexual union is God's way of demonstrating to us a great spiritual truth. It speaks to us of the greatest love story ever told, of how Jesus Christ gave Himself for us and is intimately involved with and loves the Church. In this framework of understanding between two growing Christians, the sexual relationship can become a time of intimate fellowship as well as delight. Lest there be any question as to the sanctity of sexual fulfillment in marriage, the writer of Hebrews refers to the marital bed as "undefiled." (Hebrews 13:4 KJV)

Scripture teaches sex outside marriage is wrong, sinful and destructive. However, sex in marriage is wonderfully right. It is not enough to attack the hedonistic values of secular humanism. Certainly we must stand against evils of immorality rampant in society. But we also need adequate models. We need to teach that Christian couples who are totally committed to Jesus Christ find security in physical oneness. But we must also show the world that Christian marriage works. There is no substitute for happy, fulfilling marriage relationships which serve as beacons of hope in a lost world.

Law and Government

Humanist Manifesto I: "The separation of church and state and the separation of ideology and state are imperatives. The state should encourage maximum freedom for different moral, political, religious and social values in society. It should not favor any particular religious bodies through the use of public monies, nor espouse a single ideology and function thereby as an instrument of propaganda or oppression, particularly against dissenters. People are more important than decalogues, rules, proscriptions, or regulations. We look to the development of a system of world law and a world order based on transnational federal government."

Humanists believe in state minus religion. Humanists of our day argue a doctrine of "separation of church and state" which would remove all Christian influence from government and private life.

Franky Schaeffer, in **A Time For Anger**, summarized well the problem generated by a humanist approach to law and government.

Schaeffer stated: "The Judeo-Christian influence on American society through the legal system and politics has declined to such an extent and so rapidly that we, as Christians, ought to be enraged. We find ourselves in a nation in which the law and indeed the so-called justice system is in such disarray as to be a mockery of the very words "law" and "justice." Today, to put it bluntly, we find a nation often frees its vicious criminals, and on the other hand, sanctions murder of the innocent unborn."

The modern doctrine of "separation of church and state" called for by humanists is used to silence the church. When Christians take a public stand on issues, humanists counter with arguments of "separation of church and state." The separation doctrine argued by humanists calls for a total separation of religion from civil government – quite the opposite of the original intent.

Humanists affirm a system of arbitrary law. Humanists believe man is basically good, and if given the right environment and social context, by reason and intelligence can formulate laws which are in his own best interest. He needs no theological or supernatural sanction for his actions.

Conversely, the Christian believes he is to apply the principles of God's law and God's revelation to all of life. Why? Because basic to Christian beliefs is the fallen nature of man. He is not inherently good. He is imperfect, his nature flawed by sin. Not only does he need the atonement of Christ, but also he needs the absolutes of the Bible to give order and direction to his life.

Christianity says man is sinful, humanists say there is no sin

Man is a sinful creature, and therefore cannot be his own lawgiver and judge. Law must come from God. Christians understand God is the ultimate governor and lawgiver. Absolute standards exist whereby all decisions affecting a society are to be measured. The founding fathers of America understood these principles.

The American colonies were greatly influenced by **Lex Rex**, a book written by Samuel Rutherford. Rutherford's basic premise was law and government must be based on the Bible, the Word of God, rather than the word of man. All men were under the law and not above it.

John Witherspoon, a Presbyterian minister, helped to weave the principles of Lex Rex into the writing of the Constitution. Witherspoon was the only clergyman to sign the Declaration of Independence. He was also a member of the Continental Congress from 1776 to 1779 and from 1780 to 1782. Many of Witherspoon's students were profoundly influenced by him and reached positions of prominence in the early years of the United States. They included a president, James Madison; a vice president, Aaron Burr; 10 cabinet officers; 21 senators; 39 congressmen; and 12 governors.

Our founding fathers took for granted God was the source of all laws, and was the ultimate governor of the affairs of men. They believed man was bound to obey the laws of his Creator.

Humanist law, however, is sociological law. That means law which has no fixed base, but is determined by what a group of people arbitrarily decide, is good for society at the time. Frederick Moore Vinson (1890-1953), former Chief Justice of the United States Supreme Court, stated well the humanist view of law. He said, "Nothing is more certain in modern society than the principle that there are no absolutes."

Christianity losing ground in law circles

Humanism resists the idea of a "higher law," favoring instead decisions of law based on pragmatic public policy of the moment. It is a system which encourages government of men rather than a government of laws.

This shift away from a Christian understanding of law threatens religious liberty. William Bentley Ball, in his paper titled "Religious Liberty: The Constitutional Frontier" says, "Fundamentally, in relation to personal liberty, the constitution was aimed at restraint of state. Today, in case after case relating to religious liberty, we encounter the bizarre presumption it is the other way around; the State is justified in whatever action, and religion bears a great burden of proof to overcome that presumption."

How is it a society in which the majority of people still identify with the Christian religion can be so dominated by secular humanist ideology concerning law? Francis Schaeffer, writing in **A Christian Manifesto**, stated the problem in terms of the judiciary. He said, "The law, and especially the courts, are the "vehicles to force" this total humanistic way of thinking upon the entire population. This is what happened.

The abortion law is a perfect example. The Supreme Court abortion ruling invalidated abortion laws in all fifty states, even though it seems clear that in 1973 the majority of Americans were against abortion. It did not matter. The Supreme Court arbitrarily ruled abortion was legal, and overnight they overthrew the state laws and forced onto American thinking not only that abortion is legal, but it was ethical. They, as an elite, thus forced their will on the majority, even though their ruling was arbitrary both legally and medically. Thus law and the courts became the vehicle for forcing a totally secular concept on the population."

What is the Christian response? The Bible has a lot to say about a Christian's relationship to government. From the very beginning, law and government were viewed as being ordained by God. God's commandments in this regard were clear. One was to be subject to the authorities, even though in some cases one might not agree with policies and view those policies as oppressive.

However, there was a dividing line. Nowhere were God's people commanded to do anything decreed by government which would cause them to break God's commandments. The Old Testament reveals how God helped his people structure governments under His leadership. When they did not, the people suffered. When they did, the people flourished, the nation was blessed.

Christians believe Romans 13 is a standard

The Christian understanding of government in Romans 13 is a government built on the Laws of God.

> Let every soul be subject to the governing authorities. For there is no authority except from God, and the authorities that exist are appointed by God. Therefore whoever resists the authority resists the ordinance of God, and those who resist will bring judgment on themselves. For rulers are not a terror to good works, but to evil. Do you want to be unafraid of the authority? Do what is good, and you will have praise from the same. For he is God's minister to you for good. But if you do evil, be afraid; for he does not bear the sword in vain; for he is God's minister, an avenger to execute wrath on him who practices evil. (Romans 13:1-4 KJV)

God has given us governments for our protection. God has ordained the state as an agent of justice, to punish wrong and protect that which is good. As long as the state does not insist on absolute authority and autonomy, then it can function well by keeping order and dispensing justice. State authority is not autonomous. It is delegated by God. When the state rejects the law of God, it forfeits its claim to authority.

In I Peter 2, we are told civil authority is to be respected and God reverenced.

> Submit yourselves to every ordinance of man for the Lord's sake: whether it be to the king, as supreme; Or unto governors,

as unto them that are sent by him for the punishment of evildo-
ers, and for the praise of them that do well. For so is the will of
God, that with well doing ye may put to silence the ignorance
of foolish men: As free, and not using your liberty for a cloke
of maliciousness, but as the servants of God. Honour all men.
Love the brotherhood. Fear God. Honour the king. (I Peter
2:13-17 KJV)

The state exists for the purpose of punishing wrong and rewarding
those who do right. If this is not the function, then the structure falls
apart. As the state fulfills its proper function, Christians are to obey the
state as a matter of conscience. (Romans 13:5)

In the New Testament, Christians were admonished to be subject to
the higher powers. But the commandment was not without qualification.
They were to render to Caesar the things that were Caesar's and to God
the things that were God's. If at some point Caesar should demand the
things which were God's or subvert the things which were God's, then
the people were to obey God rather than men. (Matthew 22:21)

Law and government must be based on principles outlined in the
Scriptures; the Word of God rather than the word of man. Man is accountable to his Creator. The laws he makes and governments he estab-
lishes are to be based on higher laws deriving from his Maker.

Christians often have "no-shows"

Where has been the Christian voice as we have moved swiftly toward
an almost totally secular, humanistic system of law? Where was the
Christian witness as humanists successfully argued a doctrine of separation of church and state, which excluded Christians from meaningful
participation in the state? Maybe we had accepted the role assigned to
us by the humanists, one in which we sit as quiet, harmless, passive
observers while society moves toward total hedonism.

But what is at stake here is whether we will remain a country accepting the Judeo-Christian concept of right and wrong, or turn our backs on centuries of progress to embrace practical atheism. Our nation will reap what we sow.

We can base our law and justice, our determination of right and wrong, on Holy Scripture (especially on the Ten Commandments and the Sermon on the Mount). Or we can base our law and justice, our determination of right and wrong, on the humanist values of our day. But we cannot do both. They are diametrically opposed to each other.

Christians are called to involvement in society. We stand at a crossroads of history. Every individual can take one of two ways. But Scripture makes it clear one of the two must be chosen.

We cannot embrace Christian truth and humanism at the same time. We can't have it both ways. If we try to mix the two, the message of Christianity is diluted and ultimately destroyed.

An earlier conclusion bears repeating. Humanists understand that Christianity and humanism are totally incompatible. But because of defective thinking, many Christians have assumed humanists feel the two can exist in harmony. It is time to shed the naive illusion that humanism and Christianity can be friends. They are natural enemies. Humanism, whether it is found in government, the classroom, the Supreme Court or the media, is anti-Christian. Humanism has no need for the church. If there is any room at all, it is only for a silent church.

What is the Christian response when government violates God's law? What should we do when "Caesar" requires the things which are God's? When the state becomes the source of all human values and the final arbiter of human destiny, what should be the Christian's reaction?

Our heritage in this country is Christian

From the very beginning of this nation, our system of law was based on Christian values. The Constitution was based on the premise there were certain "inalienable rights." The framers of the Constitution understood these rights were given by God. The founding fathers had a Christian world view. After all, who grants the rights? The state? If the state gives the rights, then the state can also take them away. No, our forefathers understood God grants the rights. The drafters of the Constitution knew they were building on a foundation undergirded by the blessings of God the Creator.

Our heritage in America is Christian. When the Revolutionary War was over, the first Thanksgiving Day was called. And it was called by Congress. John Witherspoon gave a sermon on that day. It contained these immortal words: "A republic once equally poised must either preserve its virtue or lose its liberty." For Witherspoon, and the vast majority of Americans of that day, this was the philosophy, which gave religious freedom to all. It was the same thinking William Penn had expressed earlier: "If we are not governed by God, we will be ruled by tyrants."

Christians are called to stand together in opposition to humanism.

How is it our Christian heritage has been almost totally replaced with a secular humanist view of law and government? To begin with, humanists have taken one phrase of Thomas Jefferson in which he mentioned a "wall of separation" between church and state, and with it have constructed an unconstitutional doctrine of how church and state should relate to each other in American society.

Franky Schaeffer in his book **A Time for Anger** states, "Our social institutions, through court edicts and authoritarian bureaucratic policy decisions, have been forced to expunge any vestige of the Judeo-Christian tradition which has, until recent years, been the ground on which the nation and indeed western civilization stood. In the guise of advocating 'neutrality,' secular humanists have replaced our nation's set of operating principles which derive from the Judeo-Christian tradition with another set of principles: these commit the United States to a materialistic view of truth, and have effectively established secular humanism as the only national religion."

The First Amendment has been badly abused

The original intent of the First Amendment was 1) to prevent a "Church of the United States," and 2) to keep government from preventing the free expression and exercise of religion. Yet, now to speak out on a public issue from a Christian perspective brings immediate accusations of violation of First Amendment "separation of church and state." How far we have drifted from the spirit of our forefathers.

In John 2, Jesus is shown in a violent attack on those who were conducting unholy commerce in "his father's house." No doubt a scene of shouting and cursing followed as the money changers attempted to hold their tables as Jesus went through upsetting them. Some would argue Jesus should have used persuasion. But what Jesus did was entirely in keeping with his character. Some assume our Lord is confined to the image of "gentle Jesus, meek and mild."

It is true Jesus loves and forgives. And true enough, He is described as "meek and lowly of heart." (Matt. 11:29 KJV) But that is not the entire picture. Through this incident we see another side of His nature. Jesus does not regard sin lightly. In reference to Herod, He said, "Go tell that fox" (Luke 13:31 KJV) He told some of the falsely religious Jews they were worldly, that he would "judge" them, and they would "die in their sin." (John 8:21-26 KJV)

Again, no one disputes that Jesus was loving and forgiving. But he also condemned sin and evil wherever it was found. It was not the loving and forgiving statements made by Jesus which took him to the cross. What the Pharisees could never abide was his strong condemnation of their sin.

Scripture is filled with examples of Godly men who did not shrink from boldly confronting sin. John the Baptist was imprisoned and ultimately lost his life after confronting Herod Antipas with the sin of adultery.

But too often when the silent church is faced with these conflicts, it weakens and wilts from humanist pressures. This was certainly not the position of the early Church.

As Francis Schaeffer writes in **A Christian Manifesto**: "The early Christians died because they would not obey the state in a civil matter. People often say to us the early church did not show any civil disobedience. They do not know church history. Why were the Christians in the Roman Empire thrown to the lions? From the Christian's viewpoint it was for a religious reason. But from the viewpoint of the Roman State they were in civil disobedience, they were civil rebels. The Roman State did not care what anybody believed religiously; you could believe anything or you could be an atheist. But you had to worship Caesar as a sign of your loyalty to the state. The Christians said they would not worship Caesar, anybody, or anything, but the living God. Thus to the Roman Empire they were rebels, and it was civil disobedience. That is why they were thrown to the lions." At one time, the church was illegal in the Roman Empire. In order to survive, it had to go underground. Their action constituted rebellion. It was against the law.

Jesus and the early Christians were not pacifists

Attorney John Whitehead, writing in **The Second American Revolution**, stated: "A popular myth invoked by Christians and non-Christians alike to justify their refusal to stand against immoral state acts has been the assertion that Jesus and his apostles were pacifists. This is not true. The question of pacifism did not arise, but Jesus was certainly not silent. He felt free to criticize not only the Jewish civil leaders.... but also the Roman-appointed ruler.... Jesus whipped the money changers and chased them out of the temple (John 2:13-17 KJV) And Christ is ultimately portrayed in the Book of Revelation as exercising righteous vengeance on the secular humanistic state.

Remember Acts 5:29? The disciples were beaten and commanded not to preach Jesus. But in Acts 5:42 we see "daily" they were preaching and teaching Jesus Christ. They could not be stopped. And what they were doing was against the law. In response to the charges of preaching in the name of Jesus, Peter replied, "We must obey God rather than men." (Acts 5:29 KJV)

The history of Christianity is filled with heroes of the faith who protested illegitimate acts of civil government. But such is not the case today. Silence of the church is interpreted as endorsement for all the state does. But it is treason to God. Scripture states, "Like a muddied spring or a polluted well is a righteous man who gives way to the wicked." (Proverbs 25:26 KJV)

Christians are called to individual and collective action. We must rediscover "active faith." The apostle James tells us, "Faith by itself, if it is not accompanied by action is dead." (James 2:17 KJV) It is a dead faith which leads one home to the easy chair when the battle for Christian values is out in the street, in public life. True faith involves commitment to action. Before David went out to meet Goliath, he said, "The battle is the Lord's." But David did not go home leaving the Lord to fight the battle. David went. David fought. David won. Why? Because he knew God was with him, God would assist him; God would strengthen him, but he himself would have to commit to the battle.

In Matthew 5, Christ says Christians are to be "the salt of the earth. " Salt preserves. If the church fulfills its role, it will act boldly to preserve Christian truth and Christian values in society. It is God's cultural mandate that Christians become involved and influential in the entire community.

What can Christians do specifically to stem the tide of humanism in society?

1. Develop a working knowledge of the issues. You can find much good material on the Internet. Many fine books have been written on the issues addressed in this study.

2. Keep informed on current legislation affecting your community, state and nation. Write and call your congressman concerning proposed legislation which you favor or oppose.

3. Become actively involved in local community affairs, politics

and legal battles for community standards. Change must start at the local level.

4. Vote.

5. Know what your children are being taught in school. Check textbooks. Values Clarification courses in many schools teach children to question their religious beliefs, as well as the teachings of their parents. Humanism is the basis for the "moral" education in the Values Clarification system.

6. Make sure your children are being taught Christian truth at home. Church is not enough. Children must be taught that Christian values apply to all of life. They need constant instruction in order to be able to overcome humanistic influences all around them. Especially critical these days is Christian instruction on human sexuality.

7. Face the issues with faithful optimism. We have God's promise that "All things work together for good, to those who love God, to those who are called according to his purpose." (Romans 8:28 KJV) Christians are to be optimistic in the battle, knowing God is working through us for the good of the church. Christians must once again become involved in every arena of public life: politics, law, medicine, higher education, science, the media, and the arts. How else can we fulfill our purpose of being the "salt of the earth?"

8. Join and support American Family Association, a national organization fighting the battle. American Family Association, P.O. Drawer 2440, Tupelo, MS 38803, phone 662-844-5036, www.afa.net.

More about humanism and public educaction

Not only did John Dewey, the father of progressive education sign the manifesto, but so did C.F. Potter, who wrote *Humanism, A New Religion*, in which he wrote, "Education is thus a most powerful ally of humanism and every American public school is a school of humanism. What can the theistic

Sunday School, meeting for an hour once a week, and teaching only a fraction of the children do to stem the tide of a five-day program of humanistic teaching?

The title of Potter's book is appropriate, because in *Torcaso vs. Watkins* the Supreme Court listed secular humanism as a nontheistic religion. Furthermore, the American Humanist Association's (AHA) own description in the **Encyclopedia of Associations** says the AHA "certifies Humanist counselors, who enjoy the legal status of ordained pastors, priests and rabbis."

Is there a battle occurring in the public schools between the religion of secular humanism and the Judeo-Christian ethic? In the magazine *The Humanist* is an essay by John Dunphy, in which he proclaimed that "the battle for humankind's future must be waged and won in the public classroom…between the rotting corpse of Christianity … and the new faith of humanism … and humanism will emerge triumphant."

Likewise, in *The Humanist*, secular humanist Paul Blanshard wrote: "I think the most important fact leading us to a secular society has been the education factor. Our schools may not teach Johnny to read properly, but the fact that Johnny is in school until he is 16 tends to lead toward the elimination of religious superstition. The average child now acquires a high school education, and that mitigates against Adam and Eve and all other myths of alleged history."

APPENDIX 2
It Is Time to Pay the Fiddler

This speech was presented to the influential Los Angeles World Affairs Council on April 6, 1982. This speech encapsulates all the arguments made against me and the issues which were being discussed in 1982.

ఆశీ

It is no accident our country is the most violent country in the entire world. It is no accident that in our country during the past seven years more than 8 million unborn babies — the weakest, most helpless, most innocent, most defenseless of all human life — have been killed. It is no accident the divorce rate and the breakup of families in our nation have skyrocketed during the past generation and nearly one of every two marriages will end in divorce. It is no accident the existence of the family — the backbone to any civilized society — as the central unit in our society is now threatened. It is no accident teenage pregnancies have become a national concern. It is no accident we are afraid to walk the streets of our cities at night. It is no accident we lock our homes, not only at night, but during the day also, or each of us have our car keys in our pocket at this very moment.

Years ago a simple Jewish tentmaker spoke these words, "Whatsoever a man sows, that will he also reap." That truth is as valid for a nation as it is for an individual. The truth of the words of Paul of Tarsus is evident in our country today. For more than a generation now our society has been sowing seeds which are today bringing forth their fruit. Truth can be rejected, but it cannot be avoided.

Things don't just happen

No, things don't just happen. One of the most elementary of all scientific truths is the law of cause and effect. Things are caused to happen. Put a lighted match in an empty gasoline can and you will have an explosion. It is a scientific, undeniable truth. Truth is as much a part of the makeup of man as it is the environment in which man lives. Teach a child to cheat to secure his goal, and he will do so until he is taught to do otherwise.

For a generation now, our society has been taught, subtly but effectively, that one's religious faith was a personal and private matter of little practical value and should not interfere with one's daily living. Recently the chairman of the board of one of the largest companies in America, a company whose sales run in the billions annually and which employs nearly one hundred thousand people, wrote me. "The Ten Commandments and the Sermon on the Mount are vanished Americanisms and the situation is moving from bad to worse, except as you know, there is a core of very religious people who are becoming more fervent and active in their religion – probably as a reaction to the evil they find around them."

For nearly two hundred years our country has been guided by a strong reliance on God. Every president, from Washington to Reagan, took the oath of office with his hand on a Bible. That is not to say all Americans were religious people in the traditional sense. Indeed, they were not. Freedom of religion also meant freedom from religion, and many availed themselves of that opportunity and still do. But underneath the heart of America there was always abiding a strong belief in the guiding hand of a Divine Being. "Stand beside her, and guide her" was our song. Today belief appears to be slowly dying, pushed aside by those whose religion is self-interest and self-indulgence.

America has an anti-Christian flavor

In its place has arisen in our nation an anti-religion attitude which no one dared to predict a generation ago. So strong is this anti-religion attitude that in today's atmosphere it would be impossible for Congress to make Christmas a legal holiday; to place "In God We Trust" on our coins; to include in the Pledge of Allegiance to the flag the phrase "One nation, under God," to have a chaplain open the sessions of Congress with a prayer; or even to allow our armed services to have chaplains. If we were attempting to do those things today they would not be able to get beyond the thinking stage.

Atheism and agnosticism, with their stepchildren of humanism, hedonism, and materialism, may not be the official religions of our country, but they have become the accepted practical religion by many in key positions of influence.

It comes as no surprise this situation has created a conflict in our society. Any religion or philosophy which teaches us to use people and love things is a natural enemy of the Christian faith, which teaches us to love people and use things.

It is no accident public schools in our nation, long a backbone for a strong country, are struggling while private, religious schools — long struggling — are growing at a record rate. Those who blame racial motives for this occurrence are correct only to a minor, indeed a very minor, degree. Families are deserting the public schools only where the public schools have deserted the families. Caring parents want their children not only to learn to read, write and do arithmetic, but also to learn basic Judeo-Christian moral values such as honesty, fairness, politeness, patriotism, integrity, discipline, obedience to authority and kindness. And they want that education to take place in an atmosphere of Judeo-Christian moral conduct.

I find it odd that a 14-year-old must have her parents' permission to have her ears pierced, but not to have an abortion. I find it odd our government will give a 15-year-old contraceptives without the permission or knowledge of the parents, but that same 15-year-old must have a parent's permission to take a school field trip.

I find it odd, but yet revealing, that many of those who want to save the baby seal find nothing wrong with killing the unborn innocent baby human. I find it odd but yet revealing, many of those who are concerned about air pollution and water pollution will contribute generously to mind pollution.

What is our greatest threat

The greatest threat to the existence of our society today in not air pollution or water pollution, but mind pollution. For the first time in history, man has an instrument through which the masses can be effectively taught immediately and effortlessly. That instrument is television. To deny that television is a teacher and motivator is to deny reality. Businessmen do not make cold, hard business decisions based on a theory television sells. They know television sells. Knowing that, they will spend more than 13 billion dollars this year selling their products via television. But television sells more than products — it sells ideas, concepts, values, morals and those other intangibles which affect the life of every person. The greatest educational system in our country today is television, and it is run, basically, by people who could not serve as principals in the Peoria School System very long.

When Lee Rich, producer of **Dallas**, **Flamingo Road** and other programs, said he had not been to church since he was 17 and did not know a single person who goes to church (he mixes and mingles with those who are responsible for what we see on television everyday and knows them on a first name basis) it answered a lot of questions about why television ignores Christian characters or belittles Christian values.

When Robert Lichter and Stanley Rothman recently released their study of 240 media elite (including editors, reporters, and other leading personnel of the New York Times, The Washington Post, *Newsweek, Time, U. S. News & World Report,* ABC, CBS, NBC, and PBS) which stated that 86% of those interviewed never or seldom attend church and 54% do not consider adultery immoral, it answered a lot of questions about why religion is treated as it is in the media. These people serve as the "teachers" on TV!

From time to time I have read that the Coalition for Better Television is trying to impose, even force, their fundamentalist religion on everyone. This only reveals the lack of knowledge of religion by those who make the accusation. Whose fundamentalist religion are we trying to impose? Is it the Catholicism of Judy Brown? The United Methodist beliefs I hold? The independent Baptist views of Beverly LaHaye? The Mormon views of Maurine Brimhall? The Jewish views of Howard Phillips? The Church of Christ views of Lottie Beth Hobbs? Or that of any one of the more than 2,000 other groups which comprise the coalition. Which one? It has to be one because it is a scientific fact that it cannot be all of them. The theological views of those I have mentioned, all part of the Coalition, are as different as day and night.

Liberals upset over Christian involvement

The rise of the coalition has also prompted the rise of those who are responsible for what goes on television. Among the most notable and visible is Norman Lear, one of the leading producers in Hollywood and founder of People for the American Way. While he has been very critical of ministers who speak out on social issues, I feel it should be noted that Mr. Lear hired Virginia Carter, described by *Esquire* as "a fervent feminist and passionate liberal," and gave her the task of working his favorite social issues into episodes of his programs. She admitted she and Lear used the programs to advocate social positions. "I consider it a duty to serve as an advocate," Ms. Carter said. "To waste that valuable air space, I'd have to be crazy." And while Mr. Lear complains about ministers who have access to one or two million viewers a week, he fails to note that the National Association for Better Broadcasting stated in 1976 that Lear "talks" by television to more people each week than any other person in history." At one time as many as 150 million man hours were spent [by TV viewers] each week watching Mr. Lear's programs and listening to his social "sermons." Mr. Lear's method of "talking" in his programs is simply another way of "preaching" as Virginia Carter so well noted. Mr. Lear, the gentleman who espouses "pluralism" called the people of Peoria, Illinois, "provincial" when they supported their television station's decision not to air his controversial **Maude** abortion episode. He received the Humanist Arts Award from the American Humanist Association in 1977.

Mr. Lear finds it acceptable for some groups to use force to change television in their own mold. Speaking about Action for Children's Television, he said, "They forced their way on the networks. They forced the networks to be attentive. … [T]hey've done that in the healthiest manner that is totally consistent with the spirit of liberty in this country." But he has been very critical because many Americans are practicing one of the most fundamental rights afforded us, the privilege of spending our money where we please.

Norman Lear moves to the front in the fight

The head of Action for Children's Television, Peggy Charren, on the other hand, has been lobbying in Washington for years to get the FCC (Federal Communications Commission) and the FTC (Federal Trade Commission) to impose Action for Children's Television's views about television on the public by government fiat. (Law) Who is it that is practicing censorship? The group practicing their right to buy or the group trying to impose their views on the public by official government action.

The Coalition for Better Television works on the following premise: "The networks can show what they desire, the advertisers can sponsor what they desire, and the viewers can view any of the choices they desire. (Only the networks and local stations tell you what you can and cannot watch and consumers can spend their money where they desire). Our entire program is voluntary. No one has to participate who does not desire to do so."

The Coalition's boycott of RCA/NBC is an exercise of stewardship, not censorship. The accusation that the boycott is censorship makes as much sense as NBC entertainment president Brando Tartikoff's recent charge that the boycott was "the first step toward a police state…" (Yes, he actually said that.) Mr. Tartikoff seems to think the republic will fall unless we continue to financially support what many of us feel is offensive and destructive programming. Our republic existed long before television turned to vulgar and tasteless programming.

We are left with the opinion from the networks that we are under an obligation to support that which we find to be morally offensive or mentally insulting. Our message is that we are not. Supporting vulgar or tasteless programming is no more our obligation than it is an obligation for this country to support economically the government of Russia.

What do those in the media really approve

What is it about me the networks and Hollywood really object to? They say it is my methods, methods that encourage people to practice selective buying as well as selective viewing. But that is only an intentional diversion. It isn't my methods that they object to. No. If it were my methods, they would have criticized other organizations which use the same methods. For instance, when the

NAACP threatened to boycott films that did not use Blacks behind and in front of the camera, there was no righteous repudiation coming forth from New York and Hollywood, no charges of censorship or police state beginnings. When I said that we would have a boycott, *The Hollywood Reporter's* front page headlines screamed in big bold black letters, "Rev. Wildmon on the Rampage Again: New Boycott Threatened."

When NAACP head Benjamin Hooks threatened a boycott, there were no headlines which read, Benjamin Hooks On the Rampage Again: New Boycott Threatened. When the Directors Guild of America announced their boycott of states which had not ratified the ERA, (Equal Rights Amendment) there were no big headlines calling the boycott unfair or repressive or screaming, "Directors Guild of America on Rampage Again: To Boycott States Which Have Not Ratified ERA." When the "Oral Majority" (not a misprint – a homosexual organization) announced a boycott of Procter & Gamble because of that company's withdrawal from 50 programs they found not suitable for their ads, there were no holy cries of censorship, no headlines which read: "Homosexuals On Rampage Again: Boycotting Procter & Gamble Because P&G Follows Policy on TV Sponsorship." No, it is not my methods that the networks and Hollywood object to. They have proven that. What, then, is it?

Gene Mater, vice president of policy, CBS-TV, expressed what they find objectionable about me in a debate we had in this city nearly a year ago. When I asked Mr. Mater why it was right for other groups, including the homosexuals, to do the same thing I was doing and not me, Mr. Mater replied: "The difference – is the fact that you are … cloaked in this self-assumed aura of religious respectability." Therein lies the problem. It is not my methods but my ideas that represent a threat. Which ideas? Ideas that spring directly from my Christian faith. That is what the networks and

Hollywood find dangerous. This was further brought out when James Rosenfield, president of CBS network, referred to me in a speech at Monterey as the "Ayatollah of the religious right." So, then, it is my ideas which must be suppressed. Ideas, you see, can be dangerous. Those who publicly accuse me of censorship are practicing exactly that of which they accuse me. They censor out the ideas I espouse, because they find these ideas dangerous.

These ideas are not new

This is nothing new. These ideas I hold have been dangerous for two thousand years. They were so dangerous that the Person to first advocate ended up on a cross, crucified by the power brokers of His day. Ideas so dangerous that for nearly 300 years the Roman Empire threatened to kill and indeed did kill those who held them. Ideas so dangerous that in Soviet Russia in this century more than 12 million people have been put to death because they held them (a fact one would never learn watching network news). Ideas considered so dangerous that in one third of the world, they are still outlawed and forbidden. Ideas so dangerous Hollywood and the networks find they must be suppressed and censored out.

What are these ideas? To begin with, the idea that man is more than an animal, that man is created in the image of God. That, indeed, is a dangerous idea. Let a person begin to conceive of himself as being infinitely important, created in the image of the Creator of the earth, and he behaves differently. He becomes a new creature. He seeks a better way. He opposes exploitation and greed. He might even dare to upset the status quo.

What kind of ideas is there that I have that are dangerous? The idea that says sex is a beautiful gift given by God to be shared between husband and wife, not cheap and vulgar like the networks and Hollywood make it. That is a dangerous idea. Should it be allowed to catch hold, then all the pornographers, from Hugh Hefner on down, and many of the filmmakers would suffer monetary loss.

What kind of ideas? The idea that says violence is not God's way of resolving conflict. Surely that is a dangerous idea. If it is allowed to spread, the public might reject a steady diet of violence on the screen and in the news. The job of Hollywood and the networks would thus be complicated. Some imagination, creativity and objectivity might be called for.

What kind of ideas do I hold are dangerous? The idea that the elderly are an important part of society, to be honored and respected for their wisdom and experience. That is dangerous. The networks and Hollywood depend on youth, primarily female youth, which they can exploit. To see beauty as something intrinsic, rather than meat well-proportioned on human bones, is dangerous. Writers might have to use creativity and imagination to bring forth suitable scripts. Presenting a half-naked female would no longer be considered an art. Females might have to be treated as intelligent humans instead of sex objects.

What kind of ideas? The idea that intelligent and thoughtful people can express themselves without resorting to vulgar, crude and filthy language. That is dangerous. If the networks should ever have to face that idea from the public, they would have to use skill to get across a forceful point.

We are moving toward a socialist, godless nation

What kind of ideas? The idea capitalism, nurtured by Christian ethics, is the finest economic system ever devised. This idea is so rejected by Hollywood that Jim Brooks, a TV writer and former producer of **The Mary Tyler Moore Show**, said concerning businessmen: "They are all sons-of-b-----." Douglas Benton, another successful writer and producer, put forth his idea of capitalism nurtured by Christian ethics.

"We are inevitably moving toward socialism. Ultimately it will come to socialism, because it's the only governmental organization which attempts to take care of the dumb and the weak and the helpless. The free enterprise system is set up to reward your energy."

The Media Institute released a study which reported 67% of businessmen on TV are depicted in a negative way and reported: "Fully three-quarters of those corporate leaders portrayed in a negative light engage in illegal activity. ... Over half of all business leaders on these primetime shows...are portrayed as criminals." It was the capitalistic system, nurtured by Christian ethics, that made this country the most prosperous in all the world and allowed us, more than any other country in history, to help underprivileged countries. Capitalism, divorced from Christian ethics, will become a most callous economic system, as socially repressive as communism.

What kind of ideas do I hold that are dangerous? The idea that religion is a vital part of life, that according to George Gallup, 90% of Americans consider themselves Christian and more than 50 million people attend worship regularly. That the Christian faith has helped build schools and hospitals, house the homeless, feed the hungry, heal the broken home, heal the alcoholic and play a central role in making this country the greatest on earth. That is such a dangerous idea, that it should not be shown on TV.

So it isn't my methods the networks and Hollywood reject. They have used and approved the same methods for others. It is my ideas, my concept of man that is dangerous. They must not let these dangerous ideas spread. They may be contagious.

What kind of life will our children and grand-children have?

What is at stake in all of this goes far beyond sex and violence on television. What is at stake is whether we will remain a country accepting the Judeo-Christian concept of right and wrong, or turn our back on centuries of progress to embrace practical atheism. The kind of society our children and our children's children will live in is at stake. Our nation will reap what we sow. That is truth you can deposit and draw interest on.

We can have a society that recognizes God and His moral standards, or we can have a society that recognizes the "make-it-as-you-go" moral standards of Hollywood. We cannot, however, have both as equals. We cannot have a society where half recognize human life as precious and half recognize human life as convenience.

We can base our law and justice, our determination of right and wrong, on the Ten Commandments and the Sermon on the Mount, or we can base our law and justice on the "make-it-up-as-you-go" values of Hollywood and the networks. But we cannot have our base on both because they are diametrically opposed to each other.

Whether we reject God or affirm Him, the fact remains we are still His children and brothers together in the family of man. We can follow the example of Cain in dealing with our brothers, or we can follow that of Andrew, but we are — have always been and will always be — brothers.

You have seen the changes which have taken place in our nation in the last generation. I ask you, is our nation a safer, better, more moral, more stable society than it was a generation ago? Is the quality of life better than it was a generation ago? And if crime, drug use, divorce, abortions as convenience, pornography, apathy and similar social ills continue for another generation as they have during the past generation, will we have the kind of society you want your grandchildren to grow up in? Do we desire to proceed in the same direction morally which we have been going for the past quarter of a century? Are we ready to sell our national soul for a mess of valueless porridge? I certainly hope not.

The greatest resource America has is her people. The most precious gift in all the world is human life. The greatest good is to serve your fellowman. The greatest tragedy is the refusal of American people to get involved on behalf of those who will come after us.

A nation which turns its back on God and His moral standards will reap what it sows. That was truth 2,000 years ago. It is truth today. It will be truth 2,000 years from now, even if we reject it.

We are beginning to learn the party is over. It is time to pay the fiddler.